About this book

I've always loved paths—those that wind through woods, and those that stir the soul toward true formation.

What if formation was an invitation to walk a path of liberation—where you are free to question long-held assumptions, explore doubt and mystery, imagine and reimagine—sometimes failing, sometimes falling—but always held by compassion, gentle strength, grace, and support.

To move at the pace of curiosity. To question. To imagine. To doubt, and wonder. To be met with grace.

That's the kind of path I want to walk.

Sauntering Homeward invites you into that journey—a gentle trail shaped by earth, water, air, and fire—where well-being grows with each thoughtful step.

SAUNTERING HOMEWARD

SAUNTERING HOMEWARD

A PILGRIMAGE TOWARD WHOLENESS
AND COMPASSION

LARRY GREY MITCHELL

FIELD NOTES

FOR SKEPTICS, SCOFFLAWS, SOJOURNERS, SEEKERS AND SOMETIME SALTY SAINTS

To my mother Lois for showing me how to walk and see with open heart and mind; and my Big Gramps James for showing me how to weep and be a light...you continue to inspire me to be ALIVE!!!

THE WORLD WILL NEVER
STARVE FOR WANT
OF WONDERS;
BUT ONLY FOR WANT
OF WONDER

G.K. CHESTERTON

TRAIL MAP

Air

Fire

Trailhead Offerings

Between my first and second years of college my dad and I walked across Scotland.

He had taken me camping plenty of times as a child. We had been on lots of day hikes (some pretty epic ones, in fact), but this was my first experience of long-distance backpacking. Our trail spanned over 200 miles of the Southern Uplands, and we had a couple of weeks to do the walking.

Heading into the trek I didn't really know what sort of daily mileage we could expect to cover. I knew that my Grampy Mitchell—dad's dad—who walked three miles a day religiously right up until the end, did so in precisely 51 minutes. I knew what it felt like to try and keep up with his refined pace on paved roads and level paths. I did not know, however, what a full pack and the Southern Upland terrain would require of us.

Our first day we set out and hiked hard, so that we could lay down a baseline. We checked the map at the end of the day and found that we had walked over 20 miles. We didn't need to cover that much ground each day, so we scaled our pace back after that and soaked up 10 or 15 miles of countryside each of the remaining days.

I was beginning to learn something about pace, and not just about the mechanics of pace, but about the spirituality of pace.

Midway through our trek, dad and I met another backpacker crossing through in the opposite direction. We stopped for a little while to talk with him while we all leaned up against a low stone fence and watched some sheep graze nearby. I still remember it vividly because it was the first time I recall ever encountering someone with an articulated philosophy of the trail.

It was simply this: Slow down. Take longer.

He spent his holidays walking around Scotland, he told us. This was his third time walking the Southern Upland Way. The first time he did it he completed it in something like 10 days. He whittled it up to 15 days the second time. And now, he said, he was going for a full 25 days on the trail. His approach to the trail was a crescendo of patience. He delighted in the whimsy of pause.

This one brief encounter with an unhurried pilgrim gave my young heart a sense of permission to consider doing the same. It instilled the spirit of saunter in my stride.

That was well over twenty years ago. Dad and I have walked thousands of miles together since then, none of them at much more than a saunter, and none of them in a straight line. The best trails wend and wind. The trails most worth strolling will compel you to stop and look and listen for what whispers are in the air. They wake you up to a sense of wonder and of possibility. They fill you up with more life than you knew was available, and then they turn you back home and set you free to offer that fullness back to others.

It is interesting to think: Trails, by their nature, are formed when we walk them, and yet when we walk them we too are formed. On a good trail you will become more fully who you are. Or at least you can, if you are willing.

The book that you are holding is a good trail. Along its bends and turns you will encounter the wild wisdom and the passionate compassion of the author's heart that I know so intimately from our decades of walking together. Here's the thing though: Even more than *his* heart—if you are willing to be a curious and unhurried pilgrim along the way—you will freshly encounter your own.

Solvitur ambulando.

Aram Mitchell
Coach, Minister, Writer, Wilderness Guide
At the heart of all the rest a wilderness guide, taking people to places where encounter with wildness and experiences of formation flow together
arammitchell.com

The word "Pilgrimage" is used frequently these days. Generally, it is locked into a particular space and time frame. It has a beginning and an end. The "Pilgrim" often has a type of spiritual experience in this space. However, my friend of nearly 40 years, Larry, has not limited his "Pilgrimage" to a specific time and space but has made it a life-long journey toward wholeness and compassion.
In fact, his life pilgrimage is in line with the words of the Psalmist 84:5-7
"Blessed are those whose strength is in you,
hearts are set on pilgrimage.
As they pass through the Valley of Baka,
they make it a place of springs;
the autumn rains also cover it with pools.
They go from strength to strength,
till each appears before God in Zion.

The portion of the text that says "heart is set" best describes Larry. Yes, he has been on many long physical journeys that are defined as "pilgrimages" and has had significant experiences of nearness to God. He has also had pilgrimages of repentance. Pilgrimages of pain and suffering. Pilgrimages of seeking forgiveness. Pilgrimages of rejoicing. Pilgrimages seeking guidance for the future. Pilgrimages of drawing nearer to family and many more. But they all result with an open heart and mind in learning, wondering, questioning, and discovering. In fact, Larry describes in this book his discovery of himself on one such journey as "I am Curious, Creative, Compassionate, Contrarian, and Committed to calling for change in the midst of chaos, confusion, and complacency."

These very words then call for more discovery of how to achieve "change". It becomes a call for contemplation and action. Much as Jesus replied to the Pharisees who were trying to trap him in his understanding of the law. Jesus replied as written in Matthew 22:37-39 ""Love the Lord your God with all your heart and with all your soul and with all your mind. This is the first and greatest commandment. And the second is like it: 'Love your neighbor as yourself."

As I perused this book, I could not stop reading. I was compelled to stop, think, wonder, write and discover more of my own journey to wholeness and compassion. Then I began to think of the treasure wrapped in these pages of years and years, miles and miles, and yes hours and hours of "inward pilgrimage". The many thinkers, scholars, theologians, philosophers' words that are sprinkled through the book – not written to be impressive – but are part of the journey impacting Larry on the trails.

In my years of friendship with Larry, I have found that he does not just write and think, but also his heart for compassion and justice is regularly put into action. I have observed him on the street with direct friendship and assistance to the marginalized as well as working to abolish systems that continue to create injustice. All of this intertwined with personal spirituality.

Please handle this book with care as you are seeing deeply into the soul of my friend. In the process, the reader will also begin to discover the hidden gems within their own soul. It may take months to fully travel the trails with Larry, but the discovery will be joy and surprise not only personally but in your relationship with others.

Perhaps Amos, the Prophet of the Hebrew Scriptures best sums up the goal of the Trail journey,,, "Let Justice roll on like a river, and righteousness as a never-failing stream." Amos 5:24

Jo Anne Lyon
Chair and Founder World Hope International
General Superintendent Emerita, The Wesleyan Church

Larry "Grey" Mitchell was introduced to me in a professional setting when he was hired as a mentor within our organization. From the very first conversation, even in the ordinary process of onboarding, he exuded an aura of authenticity, connection, and deep compassion. It was clear he had stories to tell, yet his journey was one rifled with winding switchbacks and rugged terrain. Gray is an open book—one that speaks not just through words but through the extraordinary tapestry of stories and artwork permanently written along his arms. He shares his life with raw honesty, carrying a richness of experience that defines him as both a true pilgrim and an exceptional mentor.

Grey was in the process of working through this project when we met. My father, Dennis Hamilton, spent over 60 years contributing to the literary world with stories of his own. Recognizing a kindred spirit in Grey, I quickly connected the two. Though my father's years of writing had come to an end due to illness, his thirst for stories and connection remained strong. Grey shared pieces of this book with Dad, seeking insight and perspective from a seasoned writer. Deeply moved by the project, Dad often told me how important this book was—how it had the power to guide others along the path of wellness. Sadly, he passed away before its completion. Even in our final conversations, we spoke of Grey's mission and the significance of the stories and the path laid clearly for others to take the long journey of sauntering home.

To wonder and to wander—two of life's most precious, yet increasingly neglected privileges. In an age where answers are delivered instantly by technology, the necessity of deep thought and exploration is fading. Meanwhile, mental health challenges continue to rise, as the process of critical thinking is replaced by algorithms and digital validation. Lost to the overgrowth of distraction and external noise, individuals settle deeply into their current state, affirmed in the moment by social media, without ever questioning if they could feel better or seek answers to the unknown. The concept of "wa/ondering" is fleeting. As human beings, we have a moral obligation to grow and improve ourselves. Grey has made astounding connections marking the trails for people of all walks of life to journey toward great personal discovery. He provides the tools to re-learn to think critically, rest and reflect.

Nature is an ideal classroom for self-discovery. The wilderness requires intentional presence, reflection, and quiet. It requires calculated adjustments to pace and trust not only in ourselves, but our footing and in the immense value of losing ourselves from the distractions and weight of our everyday lives. Grey has a rare ability to serve as a guide, helping the reader blaze their own trail, rather than relying on the overgrown and worn-down paths of those who claim to know best. He acknowledges the false summits of modern life - when we are met with the facade of answers only to realize that we are not done climbing. The guidance of this book provides evidence that the wild places around us often hold the answers we seek.

Once you have walked with Grey, you will have experienced a true transformation. You will emerge with a renewed sense of confidence and purpose on this beautiful planet - like the hiker reaching the ridgeline, overlooking the path behind them, recalling and embracing the struggles as much as the beauty. Through wondering and wandering, you will feel his presence next to you, the conversation he is sharing with you through the words on the page, and a rich connection to nature as you partake in your ever-so meaningful journey.

Whitney Carriger
Director of Operations, CAMPTOWN
Favorite rock climbing route:
To Defy the Laws of Tradition (5.10a) Red River Gorge

Invitation

"Now these mountains are our Holy Land, and we ought to saunter through them reverently, not 'hike' through them."

JOHN MUIR

"We are all just walking each other home"

RAM DASS

When despair for the world grows in me..." Wendell Berry begins his poem, "The Peace of Wild Things," with this familiar sentiment. Despair and fear are unwelcome companions as we navigate life, but Berry invites us to step into places of stillness—into wild spaces where water and woodlands meet, into communion with the creatures of the earth.

I sauntered through the woods today with my dog. There's nothing unusual about that; most mornings start this way. But today was a late-autumn day of rustling leaves and crisp winds sweeping in from the river. Snowflakes danced in the air, birds called, and a heron soared above the water. A pair of squirrels chattered from their tree, and cormorants shifted from their perch to glide along the water's surface.

As I often do, I stopped to breathe deeply, to listen to my soul. For a moment, as Berry writes, "I rested in the grace of the world and was free."

Yet outside these woods, the world churned with exhaustion, outrage, anxiety, fear, discouragement, and despair—a seemingly endless storm of weariness and division, with people barely holding on, bodies tired, souls worn down. For many, it was yet another "terrible, horrible, no good, very bad day," as Judith Viorst so memorably described.

Sauntering in the woods often reminds me of a truth that feels both humbling and hopeful: Our struggles aren't new. This tension—between peace and weariness, freedom and struggle—is timeless. The story of humanity is a story of sauntering home. A story of wrestling and rest. A story of finding the strength to move a little further down the path. A story of sauntering—sometimes stumbling—towards belonging, meaning, and peace.

Pretty much every day, I leave the woods again determined to live with passion for life and compassion for creation. I take one more step toward home. And as Ram Dass reminds us, we're not walking alone—we're walking each other home.

I invite you to join me on this journey....

A Path of Exploration and Growth

I have guided hundreds of experiences that I identify as pilgrimages. By pilgrimage, I don't mean a journey tied strictly to a religious experience or confined to a specific belief system. Instead, I see it as a path of exploration and growth, nurtured by curiosity and imagination.

John Muir once suggested we should saunter through nature rather than simply hike. The word "saunter" originates from medieval pilgrims who, when asked where they were going, would reply, "À la Sainte Terre," (to the Holy Land). These sainte-terre-ers were pilgrims—not just travelers. That distinction is meaningful: A pilgrimage is an intentional journey, guided by reflection, discovery, and wonder.

A TRAIL GUIDE TO NURTURING SELF-LOVE

This book is a trail guide for such a pilgrimage. Its purpose is to help you nurture self-love—not as an end in itself, but as a foundation for compassion toward others. Through journaling, storytelling, reflective questions, and practices, we will explore what it means to live more fully and deeply.

This is not a journey of rigid answers. Instead, it's an invitation to slow down, to saunter, to listen. Regardless of your beliefs, practices, or perspectives, I believe pilgrimage engages the heart, mind, soul, spirit, and body. It's about seeking your story as it intersects with the larger story of the world around you. It's not about me telling you what to think or how to think. It's about creating space for curiosity and imagination as you wander with a posture of "I wonder."

THE JOURNEY THROUGH THE ELEMENTS

The pilgrimage path in this book will journey through the elements—earth, water, air, and fire—each paired with dynamics of wellness:

- **Earth:** Physical wellness and environmental wellness
- **Water:** Mental wellness and vocational wellness
- **Air:** Spiritual wellness and financial wellness
- **Fire:** Emotional wellness and social wellness

Wellness, as I see it, is an integrative journey of self-care—one that encompasses the physical, mental, emotional, and spiritual dimensions of life. It is a practice of living more fully, nurturing a passion for life that fosters compassion for creation and all that is created.

A MEANDERING PATH

This book is not a straight-line path. It will twist and turn, meander like a river, and sometimes even seem to end abruptly—only to open onto a new vista. Along the way, you'll encounter stories, quotes, reflections, questions, and space to journal, sketch, doodle, or simply ponder. Poems will appear as places to pause and practice and as invitations to try something new. You are free to move at your own pace, take side trails, or pause and sip from the journey as needed.

I want to be your guide without being overbearing or directive. My role is to walk with you, not to dictate your path. And yes, if I start to sound preachy, I give you full permission to set this book down and imagine giving me a good-natured kick in the...well, you get the idea.

A NOTE AT THE TRAILHEAD

I grew up in a conservative Christian environment. Over time, my wanderings and wonderings have taken me far from that heritage. While I found much of that environment unsettling (a topic better discussed over a long walk or shared cup of something warm), I've come to appreciate the curiosity and imagination sparked by exploring the life of Jesus and the Hebrew Scriptures. You'll find references to Jesus and scripture throughout this book—not as an attempt to proselytize or defend, but as touchpoints that have shaped my own pilgrimage.

And now, I invite you to wander and wonder with me. Move at your pace, guided by your perspective, shaped by your joys and your challenges. This is your pilgrimage.

CREATING SPACE FOR REFLECTION

As I've said, pilgrimage, at its core, is about stepping into a journey of reflection, curiosity, and connection. It's about creating space to wonder and wander. This isn't confined to sacred trails or religious rites—it's woven into the fabric of our lives, showing up in unexpected places and moments.

One such moment found me at dinner at the United Nations.

A CONVERSATION AT THE UNITED NATI-ONS...PERMISSION TO PAUSE

A statement like that might sound impressive, but in truth, I was a "plus one" with my wife. Around the table sat individuals with titles and accomplishments that often elevate their perceived worth. The conversation began as many do in such circles—with a display of credentials and achievements.

Eventually, someone noticed that I didn't quite fit the mold. They asked, "So, what do you do?" Without much forethought, I replied, "I'm a simple theologian. I craft and curate spaces for people to explore life and faith."

This prompted some raised eyebrows and curious follow-ups. I explained that theology isn't as intimidating or distant as it might sound. It's simply the exploration of the divine—or, more broadly, what we think about the divine. In that sense, we're all theologians. Whether we believe in God, question God, or doubt God's existence, we all wrestle with meaning, purpose, and how we relate to the world around us.

As the conversation unfolded, we talked about how life's demands often crowd out space for such reflection. I shared my passion for guiding pilgrimages—journeys where people can wonder, wander, and reconnect with themselves, others, and the sacred in all things. The idea resonated. Enthusiasm grew. Yet beneath it lay a thread of sadness—a shared longing for space, time, and permission to pause.

AN INVITATION TO BEGIN

This book is an offering to meet that longing. It's an invitation to step away from the table and into a journey.

Ponder for a moment:

- Do you wander and wonder about life, faith, purpose, or place?
- Do you feel life as a swirl of hmmms, mmmms, grrrrrs, owwwws, ahhhhs, wowwwws, of curiosity, doubts, discoveries, and mysteries?
- Are you evolving in how you explore and relate to the world around you?

- Do you carry both the dreams and disillusionments that make us human?
- Do you dream to make life and the world at least a bit and sometimes even a whole lot better?

If any of this resonates, this trail guide is for you. It's more than paper and ink—it's a space for you to slow down, notice, and explore. It's a trail guide to help you traverse the pilgrimage of becoming more alive.

Imagine a pilgrimage: a path, a passage, an invitation to explore. Will you take the pilgrimage? Let's begin...

THE ART OF PILGRIMAGE

Pilgrim...
Seeking to pause and listen to my heart, my passion, and my dreams, and then to look beyond myself—reaching over my walls of comfort.

Pilgrim...
Breathing in life deeply enough to truly sense, feel, and weep; knowing it may hurt yet will nurture my soul.

Pilgrim...
Embracing challenge, risk, and epic adventures; accepting the invitation to battle indifference, make dynamic discoveries, and welcome invading grace.

Pilgrim...
Resisting the seduction of safety and the comfort of building barriers, boundaries, and borders in my life and actions.

Pilgrimage...
A path of pondering, perspectives, and practices in an intentional time of exploring and experiencing life.

A Few Reminders At The Trailhead

A t the trailhead, when starting a pilgrimage or at the start of each day when breaking camp, it's good to check in on a few basics. Enough water? Leaving no trace? Packs adjusted? At the risk of being redundant, here are a few reminders to carry with you as you step forward...

A STAR'S FIRST STUMBLE: TAKE ROADS LESS TAKEN

When I was five years old, I was a child TV star. Granted, it was in a very small galaxy, but for two weeks, I shone. I appeared on the Moncton, New Brunswick local production of Romper Room, a syndicated TV show aimed at preschoolers.

Miss Phyllis, the host, guided eight children through games, songs, and moral lessons. Each broadcast ended with a magical moment: She looked into her "magic mirror" and called out the names of children she saw in "television land." For a five-year-old, it was enchanting.

But my starring moment was also my first intentional act of rebellion or exploring my own drumbeat. During a game of "Follow the Leader," I went off script. I led my friend Boyd into hopping on one foot instead of following Miss Phyllis's bunny hops. It ended in a tumble, but the thrill of taking a different path stuck with me.

This pilgrimage invites you to explore your own roads less taken. Hop on one foot when others hop on both, even if it means the occasional fall.

A YOUNG EXPLORER'S FIRST JOURNEY: EMBRACE THE QUESTIONS AND MYSTERY

At six years old, I embarked on my first real adventure—a city hike with friends. Armed with uncooked macaroni, a flashlight (though it was mid-morning), and a map of Canada (close enough), we explored downtown Moncton and returned triumphant.

Since that day, I've walked thousands of miles in both backcountry and front country wilderness exploring questions of life itself. Preparation matters—like choosing wool socks over cotton—but I've also realized that some questions matter more than answers.

Should you sing or whistle while you walk?

Which songs should you choose?

Your choices might be influenced by where you walk, and that's okay. Sometimes, the answers emerge as you journey. Don't shy away from the hard questions or uncertain paths. They often hold the most valuable lessons.

AN EXERCISE ON THE TRAIL: CULTIVATE THE DISCOVERIES

On a recent hike with my son Aram, we discussed identity and the moments we stumble into imposter syndrome. He suggested an exercise:

List 8–10 people whose voices on life and faith I admire.

Identify 4–5 qualities I value about them.

Through this, I discovered qualities in myself that I hadn't fully owned: curiosity, creativity, compassion, and contrarian thinking. These became part of my personal declaration:

I am Curious, Creative, Compassionate, Contrarian, and Committed to calling for change in the midst of chaos, confusion, and complacency.

This pilgrimage invites you to discover and embrace the values that define your being. Take time to cultivate and curate those qualities as you walk through life.

THE INVITATION TO REST: CELEBRATE BEING

"Are you tired? Worn out? Burned out on religion? Come to me. Get away with me and you'll recover your life. I'll show you how to take a real rest. Walk with me and work with me—watch how I do it. Learn the unforced rhythms of grace. I won't lay anything heavy or ill-fitting on you. Keep company with me and you'll learn to live freely and lightly."

Jesus (paraphrased)

In a culture conditioned to expect answers, we often miss the beauty of better questions. As Parker Palmer reminds us, answers can delay growth, while good questions open us to discovery.

This book is not a map filled with answers but a companion to help you wonder and wander. Life isn't always a straight path. Some trails demand "doing"—clear, structured steps. Others invite "being"—uncertain, imaginative, and open to discovery. Both are essential. However, a valuable word to embrace as a posture on this pilgrimage is the simple BE. Let who you BE guide how, why, what, when, where you DO.

BECOMING CREATURES OF SPLENDID GLORY...BE CURIOUS

The world we live in is filled with intense expressions of selfishness that bring an evil manifested in greed, hatred, and destruction. The world we live in also is filled with incredible expressions of selflessness that bring hope, healing, mercy, and inspire us to love and live full. In *Mere Christianity*, C.S. Lewis describes how, each day, we become creatures of splendid glory or unthinkable horror, shaped by the choices we make. This pilgrimage is about choosing splendid glory—living with trust, flexibility, interruption, grace, and discovery.

Imagine a space that nurtures exploration, where curiosity replaces control, and awe supplants the desire for certainty.

Let's step out together and embrace the wonder and mystery of your story as it weaves into the larger tapestry of life.

So, as I like to say each day as we break camp...

"IT'S A GOOD DAY FOR A WALK."

TRAIL 2

Of Blackwing Pencils, Doodles, and Open Spaces

"Every time you sharpen your favorite pencil to write in your journal, you are reconfiguring minerals and wood to put them to use in bringing abstractions into expression on a sheet of pressed fibers."

ARAM MITCHELL

THE GIFT OF OPEN SPACES

As you leaf through the fieldnotes, you'll notice two things. First, there are open spaces waiting to be explored—not by predetermined answers, but by your words, doodles, sketches, thoughts, and heart. Second, those spaces intentionally remain free from blanks that demand a specific answer.

Life often requires clear answers in education, work, or decision-making, and that has its place. But this is a different kind of moment—a both/and moment. While workbooks serve us with structured blanks to fill, too little of life is spent exploring the abundant, creative fullness of simply being alive.

These open spaces invite you to ponder your story as it intersects with the stories of others—stories of creation, imagination, redemption, adventure, and restoration. They offer a place for you to slow down, reflect, and engage with your own life in the space and pace of story and community.

WHY A PENCIL?

Feel free to use these spaces however you wish— in ways that work or play for you. And as you do, I invite you to use a pencil. This, too, is intentional. A pencil invites a sensory experience while exploring your story. There's something grounding about holding it in your hand, hearing the scrape of lead on paper, and seeing the unique character of your handwritingsketchingprintingdoodling...ALIVE!!!

If you're feeling adventurous, treat yourself to a Blackwing 602 pencil. I won't tell you why it's special—that discovery is yours to make. But trust me, you deserve to experience it.

YOUR MARK MATTERS

Whether you use a Blackwing pencil, a favorite pen, or even a crayon, your distinct markings are a testament to your individuality. You are a unique creation, made in the image of the Creator, with creativity, imagination, and possibility coursing through your veins and flowing out through your fingertips.

But this isn't a call to individuality for its own sake. Instead, it's an invitation to nurture selflessness and compassion. Your handwriting—unlike a digital font—cannot be replicated. Similarly, your life is one-of-a-kind, a gift to be poured into a world that needs your unique passion and compassion.

This pilgrimage is an invitation to walk through life with a compassionate heart and generous spirit. It will be a journey of anticipation, longing, questions, wonder, courage, missteps, fear, joy, tears, laughter, rest, and wrestling. It will engage every part of you: hands, feet, eyes, ears, heart, mind, soul, and spirit.

QUESTIONS FOR REFLECTION

Take time to sit with these questions. Write, doodle, or simply ponder. The open spaces are yours to fill.

As I step onto this path, what stirs in me?

What brought me here?

What is my starting point?

Where do I hope I am going?

What support do I need as I navigate life's obstacles, opportunities, mundane moments, and magnificence?

What strengths and gifts do I bring to the journey?

CHARACTERS WHO SHAPE ME, PEOPLE WHO INSPIRE ME

A fictional character I admire (from movies, TV, or literature)—why?

A fictional character I identify with—how?

A historical figure I admire—why?

A historical figure I identify with—how?

Refer back to the people you thought of above.
What questions would I ask them?

What conversations would I like to have?

WHAT LEGACY WILL I LEAVE?

What do I want to be known for?

What is truly worth living for—not just for a time, but for a lifetime?

SOURCES OF LIFE AND JOY

Passions: What activities, plans, or dreams strengthen my heart and resolve?

Places and Spaces: Where do I feel a sense of well-being and joy?

Playlists: What movies and songs invigorate my spirit? Take time to curate these. They are part of the tapestry of your story

Lectio Divina of Sorts

---

*"Come and find the quiet center
in the crowded life we lead,
find the room for hope to enter,
find the frame where we are freed:
clear the chaos and the clutter,
clear our eyes, that we can see
all the things that really matter,
be at peace, and simply be."*

SHIRLEY ERENA MURRAY

AN INVITATION TO REFLECTION

Take some time to find the full lyrics of Shirley Erena Murray's "Come and Find the Quiet Center." After you explore the thoughts below on Haggadah and Lectio Divina, try practicing these reflective approaches using her song. Read the lyrics slowly, more than once. Let the words and their spirit settle in your heart and mind. Walk with them. Sit with them.

This song invites us into an ancient rhythm of reflection—rooted in the practices of Haggadah and Lectio Divina. These approaches encourage an *I wonder* posture, blending curiosity and reflection.

THE PRACTICE OF TELLING (HAGGADAH)

Haggadah is the art of storytelling, where passages of sacred writing or meaningful narratives are retold to guide reflection and practice.

Think of it as revisiting a favorite show, song, or story—not for judgment ("I like it" or "I don't like it"), but to let the layers reveal themselves over time and to let the feel of the words embrace you. It's about walking with the piece and letting it offer companionship and insight on your journey.

Begin with the lyrics of "Come and Find the Quiet Center." Read them slowly. Imagine retelling the story they weave. Let their rhythm and meaning deepen as you return to them.

THE FOUR STEPS OF LECTIO DIVINA

1. READ (Lectio)

Read the lyrics once, gently. Let the flow and structure unfold like the lay of the land before you. Without trying too hard, pay attention to words, phrases, or ideas that naturally stand out without being forced.

2. REFLECT (Meditatio)

Read the lyrics again—slowly, without analysis or overthinking. It's not a test. Gently let the words, phrases, and concepts "walk" with you and settle into your space. If the first reading is taking a bite of really good food, this reading is taking your time to slowly chew and let the flavors and texture emerge. Savor it rather than quickly swallowing it. What emotions, thoughts, or challenges does the song bring to you?

3. RESPOND (Oratio)

This step invites conversation, not study. With eyes open, mind and heart engaged, read the lyrics once more. Slowly still. Wandering and wondering. Let the song "speak" to you, to settle into your being. What does it call you to today? Is there a challenge, insight, or next step it offers? Consider writing down your reflections—a takeaway, an idea, or even a small action.

4. REST (Contemplatio)

Finally, pause. There's no need to read again. Instead, sit with the presence of the song in stillness. Take a few deep breaths. Let the insights settle, like food digesting, before you dive back into the rush of life.

LECTIO DIVINA PRACTICE

"Understand, I am always trying to figure out what the soul is, and where hidden, and what shape—...

I believe I will never quite know..."*

MARY OLIVER, "BONE"

Find Mary Oliver's poem "Bone" (not to be confused with her "Bone Poem"). As with the song, read it slowly, more than once. Let her words percolate in your heart and mind. Walk with them. Sit with them. Practice some Lectio Divina with them.

You might find the practice of Lectio Divina helpful here as well. Let the poem guide you to new insights. What does it reveal about your journey, your questions, and the quiet spaces within?

MUSIC FOR THE JOURNEY

If we could walk a wilderness trail or a city sidewalk together, we might share songs and poems to spark curiosity and wonder. Whether under the stars in a desert canyon or on the grass in a bustling city park, we would listen—not just to the music, but to the silence, the thoughts, and the stories they inspire.

Songs and poems will appear throughout this guidebook. I invite you to seek them out, listen deeply, and discover where they lead you.

One song I encourage you to explore early in this pilgrimage is "Guiding Light" by Foy Vance. Find the song. Listen to it several times. Let its words and spirit percolate in your heart and mind. Walk with it. Sit with it. Practice some Lectio Divina with it.

And for some additional sensory experience, see if you can find the YouTube video of the song with Foy Vance and Ed Sheeran.

TRAIL 4

Once Upon a Time in the Beginning... Chaos and Creation

"Truly, we live with mysteries too marvelous to be understood..."

MARY OLIVER

THE GENESIS OF CREATION

In the beginning, when God created the heavens and the earth, the earth was (tohu va bohu) waste and void; and darkness covered the face of (tehom) the deep, while (ruach) a wind from God swept over the face of the waters... Then God formed a person from the dirt of the ground and breathed into his nostrils the breath of life, so that he became a living being.

—Genesis 1:1-2, 2:7

Ancient creation stories often begin with chaos—a force necessary for the emergence of beauty, meaning, and life. In the Hebrew creation story, we see **tohu va bohu** (waste and wild), **tehom** (the depths), and **ruach** (the breath, the wind, the stirring over the waters).

As theologian Catherine Keller writes in On the Mystery, "there is no nothingness, but a whole lot of not-quite-somethingness." Creation, then, doesn't emerge from a void of nothingness but from the fertile energy of chaos—the hubbub, uproar, and swirl of astonishment. It is here, in the midst of bewilderment, that the breath of imagination and curiosity begins to stir.

CHAOS AS A CREATIVE FORCE

Across human history, mythology and ancient stories emphasize chaos as a necessary force for creation. As Matthew McKenna writes:

"Mythology and ancient stories across human cultures represent chaos as a necessary force for creation. The necessity of chaos is an idea at the core of humanity, represented in the creation myths of ancient Greece, ancient Mesopotamia, and the ancient Hebrew peoples, along with the creation myths of the Indigenous Haudenosaunee and Aztec peoples. Human stories suggest chaos is essential to the world, with chaos as the necessary precondition for creation and goodness."

When I reflect on chaos, I see confusion, struggle, and pain—but I also see it stirring musicians, poets, and playwrights to inspire us. I see it propelling scientists to find cures, explorers to discover new horizons, and philosophers to wrestle with questions of mystery and existence. Chaos compels us to create.

This connection between chaos and creativity is not only universal in myth but also deeply personal, as reflected in the Genesis story. The path from chaos to creation is one that we walk throughout life, unfolding through the transformative power of the elements.

THE PATH FROM CHAOS TO CREATION

The Genesis story begins with darkness and void but unfolds into life-nourishing elements. Eventually, ancient cultures identified those elements as earth, water, wind and fire. Each element carries the human story forward, igniting the divine spark within.

Walking through chaos invites us to move from disorientation to wisdom, from struggle to meaning. These moments, when your story intersects with the creative energy of the universe, can be sacred—where divine and human narratives meet, and transformation begins.

4 ELEMENTS OF LIFE...

Earth
Pay attention to what grounds you—practices that root you in the soil of living, anchoring you to life's physical realities. Reflect on the call to steward creation with "radah"—care and reverence for the world that holds you.

Water
Pay attention to what clears your mind and awakens curiosity—practices of reflection and exploration that nurture mental clarity. Reflect on the currents that enliven your spirit and the vocational call to bring meaningful work into the world.

Air
Pay attention to the whispers of spirit and the breath of life—practices of contemplation that deepen your faith and spiritual awareness. Reflect on the interplay of poverty and wealth, and consider how financial choices shape the paths of life.

Fire
Pay attention to what ignites your passions and compassion—practices that stir creativity, imagination, and emotional depth. Reflect on the spaces and rhythms that foster community, civility, and the bonds of neighborliness in a shared world."

SPACE AND PACE FOR WONDERINGS AND REFLECTIONS

SENSORY EXPERIENCES

Just earth and underground springs, no grasses, flowers, or shrubs...

I wonder: What did Earth look like before grasses, flowers, or shrubs existed?

I wonder: What were the sounds, colors, and smells before and after the grass, flowers, and shrubs appeared?

CREATOR'S PROCESS

I wonder: What did the dirt feel like in the Creator's hands as humanity was formed? Was there dirt under the fingernails?

I wonder: Was the process of creation instantaneous, like a snap of the fingers? Or did it unfold slowly, like a simmering stew?

I wonder: Was there trial and error? Stops and starts? Oops moments? Miscalculations that ended up being wonderful reimaginings?

I wonder: Was it a slow creative work full of imagination and spontaneous expressions of curiosity? Or carefully calculated and engineered blueprints guiding the creation? Or both?

I wonder: Did the Creator whistle while working? And did the Creator work up a good sweat?

HUMAN AWAKENING

I wonder: When the Creator blew the breath of life into the man's nostrils, was it like the wind blowing across a lake, or was it more like mouth-to-nose CPR?

I wonder: What did it feel like for the dirt to become human and for the breath to become life? Was it like waking up from a deep sleep?

I wonder: What did it feel like to experience the spark of life—what we call "fire in the gut"—turn into full flames of existence?

I wonder: What were the first moments of human wisdom or common sense? What were the first expressions of communication?

WALKING THROUGH CHAOS

Life's chaos is an invitation to step into the unknown with a sigh, yes—but also with courage. It is the space where transformation begins, where stories unfold, and where wisdom is born.

Perhaps a creation prayer could be breathed into the chaos:

"I do not know myself yet. Help me believe, help me imagine and create. Help me walk through the valley of my fears with courage."

As you walk the path of chaos and creation, consider these questions:

Where do I see beauty?

Where do I see grime—the waste and the wild?

Where do I feel grit in my life?

How might this pilgrimage transform me and my world?

Can I trust the Creator with the unknown and let the mystery be?

What do I want to be known for?

What is worth living my life for—not just for a time, but for a lifetime?

Steps Along the Path

Always in big woods when you leave familiar ground and step off alone into a new place there will be, along with the feelings of curiosity and excitement, a little nagging of dread. It is the ancient fear of the unknown, and it is your first bond with the wilderness you are going into. You are undertaking the first experience, not of the place, but of yourself in that place."

WENDELL BERRY

"Those who believe that they believe in God, but without passion in their hearts, without anguish in mind, without uncertainty, without doubt, without an element of despair even in their consolation, believe only in the God idea, not God Himself."

MIGUEL DE UNAMUNO

"The rhythm of climbing—the cadence of movement, of upward momentum—is an elusive thing, and the slightest spasm in a mental muscle can throw it off. Above all else climbers battle

for control... When these fears are eclipsed, when they are replaced by moments of control, and when that control turns into a kind of grace—that is what climbers savor and what they will remember long after a climb is finished."

MICHAEL WEJCHERT, HIDDEN MOUNTAINS

Over the years, as I have guided pilgrimages and backpacking adventures—through winding desert paths, canyon rivers, snow-covered mountain passes, urban alleyways, and pine-needle-carpeted forest trails—I've observed a rhythm in the experiences of those who join me. These experiences, though unique to each person, often have a recurring pattern of steps.The beauty of these steps is that they are cyclical; they repeat, evolve, and shape us as we walk, bringing new lessons with each turn. Let's walk through these steps and have a space for reflection.

DECISION

To step into a pilgrimage, an adventure, or a significant experience begins with a choice—a series of decisions, some big and probably mostly small, that eventually lead to a pivotal "yes" or "no." These decisions are not usually made in a single moment and not without some wrestling before reaching the moment of commitment and taking that actual first step.

Take a moment to reflect on the decisions that brought you to this point.

DOUBT

Here's the thing about decisions: Once you make them, doubt often creeps in. I have had many moments on the path (and also pre-path) when trailmates share doubts about their decisions. *Can I really do this? What if I'm not strong enough? Do I have the right gear? Is this worth my time?*

Doubts are natural. They're not something to be afraid of. But left unchecked they can sap your energy and passion. Instead of avoiding doubt, face it and allow it to lead you to the questions, even the hard ones.

Author Chris Dombrowski notes: "It is easier to nestle beneath the goose-down comforter of irony in our age of complicity than to entertain the hard questions."

DESPAIR

Let's talk about the tough part. Almost every challenging pilgrimage or adventure has moments when despair shows up.

It might be physical: *My pack is too heavy. My muscles ache. I'm wet, cold, tired, and hungry.*

Or it might be emotional: *I'm scared. I don't think I can do this. Maybe I shouldn't have come.*

I've had those moments—trudging through rain, feeling like I'm carrying the weight of my pack and the world. Despair feels heavy. But here's what I've learned: Despair may be a trail mate of doubt, but it's not the end of the road.

When despair shows up, stop, lift your head, and look around. Recalibrate focus and perspective. Let it teach you something about yourself, the path, and the next step forward.

DISCOVERY

And then, there it is—the yellow flower growing in the desert. Notice it. Notice the smile and encouragement of a trailmate. Notice the songs of the river, the birds and the wind weaving along the trail. I love the moments when a trailmate lifts their head, takes a deep breath, and they notice and discover they're stronger than they thought. Those are moments when courage returns, strength reawakens, and confidence reignites the gait and spirit. And the voice and heart shout, "ALIVE!!!"

DELIGHT

And then, delight.
That spring water was the best I've ever tasted.
That sunset was worth every step of the climb.
I'm so glad I didn't give up.

Delight is the reward for walking the path—the joy and gratitude that fills your heart when you realize the journey wasn't just about reaching the end. It's the embrace of a trailmate, the laughter around the campfire, the connection to something bigger than yourself. And it is life giving.

DECISION

How do I make decisions?

What/who, perhaps even a bit of when, where and why are the influences that guide my decisions?

DOUBT

What doubts are surfacing for me in this season of life?

What am I questioning because of the doubts?

Where are the questions leading me?

DESPAIR

What tends to bring despair or discouragement onto my path?

How do I respond when fear or despair sets in?

DISCOVERY

What gives me courage and confidence?

How do I create space and pace for discovery in my life?

DELIGHT

What are some simple things that delight me?

When was the last time I felt truly ALIVE?

TRAIL 6

Focus, Looks, and Mysteries

FOCUS ON THE JOURNEY

When I guide walkabouts and backpacking pilgrimages, I encourage one primary posture: *Focus on the journey*. It's easy to fall into the trap of seeing the trail as a race to the destination—a box to check on the endless "to-do" list of life. The temptation to conquer the path or to compete with fellow hikers can take hold, shifting the focus to the quickest, strongest, or most efficient way to get from point A to point B.

But when this mindset takes over, something essential is lost. The path becomes something to overcome rather than embrace. I've found that when I shift my focus to the journey itself, I'm more open to what the trail offers: lessons, challenges, beauty, and a deeper sense of well-being.

To nurture this mindset, I remind myself—and my trailmates—of an important practice: how we look. Not how we look to others but how we look *with our eyes*. The way we observe our surroundings while walking, both literally and figuratively, can transform our experience.

Carrying a 40-60 lb pack has a way of narrowing our gaze to the ground, watching each step for roots, rocks, and steady footing. While it's necessary to watch the path, there are other valuable perspectives to practice.

THE FOUR LOOKS

1. Practice the Look Ahead

Raise your eyes from the trail beneath your feet and look toward the horizon. The vistas ahead invite anticipation and expectation. They pull you forward, offering motivation for the next step and reminding you that every journey moves toward something.

This "look ahead" can also be a perspective on what lies beyond the trail: What are you carrying back with you? How does this experience intersect with the future you'll step into when the pilgrimage is over?

That said, there's a balance to be struck. Some horses near the end of a trail ride sense the barn and try to rush to the stable doors. They have to be reined in. Same with exploring pilgrimage. We, too, can feel the pull of the "end." It takes intention to resist that rush and remain present. The parking lot at the trail's end will still be there, and the pack will come off your back soon enough. Until then, savor what the trail has to offer.

2. Practice the Look Back

Pause and turn around. Let your gaze trace the path you've already walked. Maybe even take a few careful steps backward.

Looking back allows you to appreciate how far you've come. It's a reminder of the landscapes you've passed through, the obstacles you've overcome, and the beauty you may have missed in the moment. Seeing your trailmates hiking behind you adds another dimension—a mirror of your own journey moments before, connecting you to the shared rhythm of the path.

3. Practice the Look Up and Around

Every so often, stop—not to catch your breath, but to take in the fullness of where you are. Look up at the sky, at the towering trees, at the sandstone cliffs. Let your gaze wander wide and far, then focus on the details: the veins of a leaf, the ripple of water over stones, the shimmer of light through the canopy.

Engage all your senses. Listen to the wind, the rush of a distant river, or the profound stillness of the wilderness. Smell the pine needles. Touch the rough bark of a tree or the cool smoothness of a stone. Taste the spring water as it runs over rock.

Looking up and around connects you deeply to the moment, anchoring you in the sacred present.

4. Practice the Look Down

While the other perspectives expand your view, the "look down" keeps you grounded—literally. It's necessary to pay attention to the ground beneath your feet, to notice the opportunities and obstacles directly in your path.

But there's a balance here too. Don't become obsessed with this downward view. Practice walking with trust—trust in your footing, trust in the path, trust that you're moving forward with intention.

THE MYSTERY OF THE TRAIL

Many of my walks and hikes have included wondering conversations with Andrew Fritz, a trailmate and fellow pilgrim. As we practice the four looks, a frequent pondering he explores is the presence of mystery, woven into the trail and into life itself. Mystery is the element that challenges our comfort zones, nudges us toward the unknown, and compels us to confront both joy and despair. It's a whisper that beckons us around the next bend, promising both sustenance and challenge. To listen to the whisper and take the step, there must be intentionality.

REFLECTION: MY PRACTICE OF LOOKING

These four looks can be practiced both literally when on the trail and figuratively as you explore the fullness of life. As you consider these four ways of looking, take time to reflect on your own journey.

THE CALL OF INTENTION

What mysteries are calling to me on my current path?

What step of risk am I being invited to take?

BREAKING FREE FROM COMFORT

What comforts hold me back from embracing the unknown?

What would it mean to step beyond them?

PERSPECTIVE AND FOCUS

Which of the four looks comes most naturally to me?

Which one do I practice more intentionally right now?

ONE MORE STEP

The next time you're on a trail—or simply walking through your daily life—pause to practice these perspectives. Look ahead, look back, look up, and look down. Notice how each view reveals something new.

And as you walk, remember that mystery is part of the journey. Embrace it, trust it, and let it guide your next step forward.

Praying with Your Gut

A Prayer From The Bow Of A Boat

ARAM MITCHELL

I want to sing You a song.
But I don't have words
strong enough or music sweet
enough to honor You.

I want to paint You a picture.
But I don't have a brush fine enough
colors rich enough, or a hand steady
enough to do You justice.

I want to write You a poem.
But I don't have thoughts pure enough
or verse whole enough to
express Your majesty.

I want to give You an offering.
But I don't have animal
blameless enough, harvest
bountiful enough, gold
true enough, or incense thick

enough to make even a
dent in the debt of my gratitude.

So may I suggest (or perhaps
finally accept Your Suggestion
spoken to us an eternity
ago by a Voice hovering
over the waters and continually
spoken to us through a chosen
people, through prophetess
and prophet, through poets
and thinkers of old, and
especially and powerfully
through the Word in
Flesh, Jesus; then suggested
further by and through
His courageous followers
throughout the years)
that I simply Live.

Moment by moment let me
and help me and create within
me the desire and
strength to Live as though
singing to You at the top
of my lungs; as though
painting for You with beautiful
strokes and magnificent colors;
as though reciting to You a
poem of passion from heart;
as though offering to You
everything and beyond
everything and beyond the beyond.
I want to simply Live You a LIFE.
Amen — may it be so.

Aram's words remind us that prayer is not about perfection. It's not about offering the right words in the right way with the right posture, gestures, or gifts. Instead, prayer is a way of living—a conversation that flows through our thoughts, actions, and steps. It's an offering of ourselves: raw, honest, and fully present.

Prayer is not confined to whispered words in quiet spaces. It is expressed in our groans and sighs, in the beauty we create, in the kindness we extend, and in the paths we walk. Sometimes, it's simply silence. Sometimes, it's tears. Always, it's an honest reflection of our heart, mind, spirit, guts.

PRAYER FOR THE WALK HOME

Whether you are walking a physical trail or navigating the twists and turns of life's pilgrimage, prayer can be a guide—a companion for the journey. Take a moment to consider where you are today, where you've been, and where you hope to go. Let this reflection guide you as you write your own prayer for your path, your journey, and your life.

Here are a few prompts to help you begin:

1. A Prayer of Gratitude
What am I thankful for in this moment? What blessings—big or small—have I encountered on my path so far?

2. A Prayer of Guidance

Where do I need direction or clarity? What uncertainties am I carrying, and where am I seeking light to illuminate my walk home?

3. A Prayer of Strength

What challenges lie ahead that feel heavy or overwhelming? Where do I need courage, resilience, or peace to keep moving forward?

4. A Prayer of Surrender

What burdens, fears, or doubts do I need to release? How can I open my hands and heart to trust in something greater than myself?

Take a few moments to reflect. Then, using the space below, I invite you to write a prayer as you continue to saunter homeward. Let it be as simple or as intricate as you need. It might be a single word, a sentence, a paragraph, or a poem. It might be a song or a picture. Let your prayer reflect the honesty of where you are and the hope of where you're going.

imagination believe

inspiration collaboration

question mourn

table community

awe quest seek

receive give

mystery discover

inspire wonder

laugh   weep   despair

rejoice hope

epic   emotion   forgive

reverence   adventure

faith   reform

vulnerability

reframe

exploration   healing

conversation   curiosity

REFLECTIONS, WONDERINGS,
PONDERINGS, DOODLINGS

REFLECTIONS, WONDERINGS, PONDERINGS, DOODLINGS

REFLECTIONS, WONDERINGS, PONDERINGS, DOODLINGS

REFLECTIONS, WONDERINGS, PONDERINGS, DOODLINGS

EARTH

LECTIO DIVINA PRACTICE

"Create a clearing in the dense forest of your life and wait there patiently."

MARTHA POSTLEWAITE

Find Martha Postlewaite's poem "Clearing." Read it several times. Let its words and spirit percolate in your heart and mind. Walk with it. Sit with it. Practice some Lectio Divina with it.

TRAIL 8

Dirt Under the Fingernails

"After saying this, he spit on the ground, made some mud with the saliva, and put it on the man's eyes... They said, 'You're nothing but dirt! How dare you take that tone with us!' Then they threw him out in the street."

JOHN 9:6, 34

"Of all the paths you take in life, make sure some of them are dirt."

JOHN MUIR

THE BEAUTY OF GETTING DIRTY

I like that Jesus wasn't afraid to get his hands dirty—deep grime and grit under the fingernails dirty. As a carpenter, his hands were strong, calloused, and familiar with splinters and bruises. Those same hands shaped wood, touched lepers, broke bread, and, in this story, made mud to give a blind man his sight.

Jesus entered the mess—the questions, the struggles, the awkward pauses that come with creating space for life, transformation, and redemption.

In John 9, there's a story about a blind man, some mud, and a miracle. I invite you to read it, not as a scholar or someone searching for answers, but with the wide-eyed wonder of childhood days and have fun. Imagine being there:

I wonder what sights, sounds, smells, touches the people in and around the scene experienced?

I wonder what the blind man was thinking as his condition was debated like a theological puzzle?

I wonder what he thought when he heard the sound of spitting, the scrape of dirt, and the rustle of Jesus' robe as he approached?

I wonder what he felt as he sensed the movements getting very much into his personal space.

I wonder if the mud was cold or warm? Gritty or smooth? Was it a shock, or did Jesus' voice calm him with quiet words?

And why *mud?* Why not a simple touch or a few words?

MORE THAN JUST DIRT

"There are more living things in one teaspoon of soil than there are people on the planet."

THE JAMES HUTTON INSTITUTE, "WHAT ON EARTH"

Soil is alive. It teems with life, even when we see it as nothing more than dirt.

"Land, then, is not merely soil: it is a fountain of energy flowing through a circuit of soils, plants, and animals."

ALDO LEOPOLD

Soil also holds our history. At the Equal Justice Initiative's Legacy Museum, there is an exhibit containing 800 jars of soil collected from lynching sites across the country, each one labeled with the name, date, and story of a life lost by lynching. Bryan Stevenson, founder of EJI, says:

"In this soil, there is the sweat of the enslaved. In the soil there is the blood of victims of racial violence and lynching. There are tears in the soil from all those who labored under the indignation and humiliation of segregation. But in the soil there is also the opportunity for new life, we can actually plant something that imagines a chance to grow something hopeful and healing for the future."

This is the paradox of dirt: It holds our scars and our seeds. It is both a witness to what has been and a vessel for what *can* be.

DIGGING INTO THE SOIL

What is my relationship with the soil?

How am I engaging with the earth and its stories?

What seeds of compassion—for self, neighbor, and creation—am I planting?

What future am I imagining for myself and for the world?

Physical Wellness

"It will be solved in the walking."

ST. AUGUSTINE

FULLY ALIVE

Wellness begins with paying attention to how we live.

Jesus lived in a fully physical way. He walked pretty much everywhere. He gathered with friends around fires, worked with his hands, and enjoyed meals with laughter and wine. He withdrew to the wilderness—deserts, mountains, and lakes—to care for his well-being. He noticed birds, flowers, and farmers, weaving them into stories as invitations to pay attention. He practiced being present and aware of his physical nature and surroundings. His approach to the physical dynamic of living is a valuable prompt for us to consider the role that the physical and the environmental dynamics have in our wellness.

Let's start with what "wellness" means...

WHAT IS WELLNESS?

In health terms, wellness refers to the choices and practices that guide us toward balanced, healthy living. It sounds simple—yet it's often approached casually, treated with indifference, or ignored altogether. On the other hand, wellness can feel overwhelming, with complicated programs, lofty expectations, and rigid definitions.

But in reality, **wellness is personal**. As IncentFit, a company focused on wellness benefits, explains:

> "Wellness looks different for everyone, yet it has one
> common focus: achieving a balanced lifestyle that
> results in fuller, healthier, less stressful lives."

A wellness practice is anything that nurtures a balanced life, with each step contributing to the path of well-being.

Physical wellness often focuses on three essentials: **movement, good nutrition, and sleep**. Countless resources—books, programs, apps, and articles—offer guidance on these basics. A quick Google search reveals titles like "28 Wellness Activities Everyone Will Love" or "50 Wellness Activities: What Are They, Why Are They Important, and Examples."

Whether you dive deep into resources or keep it simple, the key is to take that first step and begin exploring what works for you. There's no magic formula—just steps to take, one at a time, in the direction of life.

AN INVITATION TO EXPLORE

Wilderness and spirituality guide Aram Mitchell writes:

> "Exploring is about finding pace at the marginal edges
> of our souls, in the busy demands of our own days,
> despite the faulty tendencies of our own culture...
> making space to practice life and become more fully
> alive."

Wellness is an act of exploration. A practice.

Am I nurturing my well-being? Am I too busy to pay attention to how I eat, sleep and move?

How am I caring for my physical well-being—how I move, eat, and rest?

What small step can I take to make space for physical wellness today?

What will I do to make space and pace to care for my life and be more ALIVE?

SOLVITUR AMBULANDO...A PHYSICAL WELLNESS PRACTICE

"Solvitur Ambulando"

"The Road goes ever on and on
Down from the door where it began.
Now far ahead the Road has gone,
And I must follow, if I can..."
– J.R.R. Tolkien

For the past few decades, I've spent an average of 347 days a year walking—through woods, deserts, snowy trails, and urban sidewalks. When I walk I'm embraced by the world around me.

I walk not to reach a destination but to make nature an everyday, ordinary experience. Walking has become an intentional practice of learning and living, subtly inspired by the imagery in Genesis of Yahweh walking—not driving or hurrying—but moving at a pace that allows for connection, discovery, imagination and wonder.

I wonder if Yahweh took regular walks in the garden with Adam and Eve. Was it part of their daily rhythm? I imagine conversations unfolding during unhurried walks. What might those walks have been like?

- Did Yahweh ever tousle Adam's hair in a playful way?
- Did Yahweh hold Eve's hand as she leapt from rock to shore while crossing a stream?
- What did the divine laugh sound like?
- What language did they use?
- And yes, what did Yahweh look like?

I like to wonder how those walks nurtured well-being for all the walkers. Did the embrace of sensory experiences with nature guide and inspire each of them?

Walking invites me to notice—to see, hear, smell, and feel the world. To slow down. To pay attention. It's a way of being present, alive to the sensory gifts that the earth offers every step of the way. When I walk I'm embraced by the world around me.

"The press of my foot to the earth brings a hundred affections."

WALT WHITMAN

WALKING PRACTICE...
HOWEVER YOU WANT TO DO IT, WALK

Amblecareenfalterfounderlimplumberlurchmeanderpara deprowlramblesaunterskipskulksomnambulatestaggers-talk stridestrollstrutstumbleswaggertottertrudge-waddlewade

WALK WITH INTENTION

Whatever walk you choose, let it be a mindful practice. Be present and attentive. Slow down. Be simple and kind—to yourself, to others, to creation. Walking offers a gentle reciprocity: the earth is kind back to you grounding you in its rhythms. Get up, get outside, and go for a walk—any walk:.

- **A moonlight walk** quiet and calm with the night sky
- **A rainy day walk**, puddles inviting playful steps washing away the weight of the day.
- **An early morning walk**, breathing in the crispness of dawn.

- **A local park walk**, surrounded by the green of familiar spaces
- **A go to the market for supplies**, where movement meets purpose.
- **A find a fallen tree to sit on for a while walk**, pausing for reflection and rest.
- **A sensory walk**, focusing on one sense at a time.
- **A curiosity walk**, letting wonder and questions lead the way.
- **A forest walk**, where trees breathe and time feels endless.
- **A beach walk**, paced by the rhythm of the waves.
- **An urban sidewalk and alley walk**, exploring the stories of the city.
- Or my favorite: **a fresh falling, deep snow, 0-degree saunter in the woods walk**, where silence and beauty embrace every step.

As you walk, be present and mindful, be slow and silent, be simple and kind...kind to yourself, others, creation. And the beauty of walking is that the earth will be kind back to you, grounding you in its rhythms.

WALKING MATTERS

The benefits of walking aren't just poetic—they're proven. A British report, *Walking Works*, highlights the transformative power of regular walking:

- Reduces the risk of coronary heart disease and stroke by **20–35%**.
- Lowers the risk of breast cancer by 20% and colon cancer by **30–50%**.
- Reduces the risk of type 2 diabetes by **35–50%**.
- Decreases the risk of Alzheimer's by **40–45%**.
- Lessens the risk of depression by **20–30%**.

So—take a step. The pace doesn't matter. What matters is making space for walking, for connection, and for life.

"Life is already too short to waste on speed. Walking stretches time and prolongs life. It makes the world much bigger and thus more interesting. You have time to observe the details."

EDWARD ABBEY

A canyon prayer
The winding path becomes a friend
With feet to earth I say my prayers
At every turn and every bend,
I surrender all my cares

How will I take my next step—toward wellness, wonder, and life?

WALKING AND EXPLORING EARTH IS AN INCLUSIVE PRACTICE

My mother had polio and MS when I was born. In my early childhood, she was mostly confined to a chair, later transitioning to a wheelchair with some ability to move her hands and arms. By my teen and young adult years, she could walk slowly with the aid of a walker or canes. Doctors gave her six months to live in her twenties, but she lived into her seventies, eventually able to take careful steps without assistance.

Though she couldn't take long walks with us, she cherished slow strolls through the tree-lined paths by the Saint John River, often holding my arm or my dad's. When walking wasn't possible, she'd have my dad help her outside to sit, watch, listen, smell, and feel the aliveness of the earth.

My friend, Sarah, was paralyzed from the chest down in a high school ATV accident. Now a wife and mother of six, she has joined me on numerous pilgrimages, navigating miles of streets in Toronto, Tijuana, and Indianapolis. Her "walking" was done in a basketball wheelchair, wheeling herself along alleys, pathways, and uneven ground. Yet, her presence and connection to the journey were as profound and complete as anyone else's.

My friend Shawn is blind. He has walked with me on pilgrimages in the same cities, as well as remote jungles and villages in Costa Rica, and even during a 17-hour mountain summit in a blizzard in the Adirondacks. On sensory walks, when I asked what people had seen during the day, Shawn often shared observations the rest of us had missed. He frequently used the phrase, "I saw," and while he experienced the world primarily through his other senses, there was no denying he illuminated details with a clarity that felt visual to us all.

I have countless similar stories about other trailmates I've walked with on pilgrimages. Perhaps I'll share more when we take a walk together.

Walking is an inclusive practice, not defined by how far or fast we go, or even by literal steps. Whether moving on foot, wheels, or confined to a bed, "walking" can be a metaphor for any intentional act of connection with the earth. Listening to the rustle of leaves, feeling sunlight on your skin, or simply breathing deeply in nature's presence can be its own kind of walk.

In whatever way you can, may you find your own trail and,

"May your trails be crooked, winding, lonesome, dangerous, leading to the most amazing views."

EDWARD ABBEY

TRAIL 10

Enviromental Wellness

Environmental wellness is about respecting, nurturing, and embracing spaces that promote well-being—spaces that are sustainable, accessible, livable, and stimulating. It encourages interaction with nature, a commitment to caring for the health of the world, and cultivating personal environments that spark passion for life and compassion for all creation.

"Why is it that the destruction of something created by humans is called vandalism, yet the destruction of something created by God is called development?"

EDWARD ABBEY

"To harm the earth is to harm man; to ruin the earth is to destroy man."

THOMAS BERRY

A BOOK OPEN TO THE SKY...THE CALL TO CARE

Environmental wellness invites us to appreciate and engage with nature through outdoor activities—hiking, swimming, camping, or simply breathing in the air of open spaces. It's also about conscious choices: reducing waste, conserving resources, recycling, and protecting the abundance of clean water, natural resources, and sustainable food supplies.

This wellness is rooted in the understanding that our well-being depends on the planet's health. To harm the earth is to harm ourselves and future generations.

When my kids were fourteen, I took each of them on a two-week Legacy Trip. They chose the destinations, and together we explored life, culture, and the outdoors. I created a collection of life principles to share, and each day, I paid attention to moments that sparked a meaningful connection to one of those principles. Both Laura and Aram chose Scotland and England, where we wandered cities, villages, woodlands, and highlands, reflecting on the past, present, and future.

"Legacy Trip Principle: Plant trees you may never get to sit under."

Environmental wellness also invites us to consider: What would the world be without the wildness and wonder we so often take for granted?

"What would the world be
once bereft of wet and wildness?
Let them be left, oh let them be left.
Wildness and wet.
Long live the weeds and the wildness yet."

G. M. HOPKINS

FAITH AND CREATION CARE

"I don't think it is enough appreciated how much an outdoor book the Bible is. It is a hypaethral book, as Thoreau talked about—a book open to the sky. It is best read and understood outdoors, and the further outdoors, the better."

WENDELL BERRY

For me, the call to environmental wellness begins with the first command given to humanity in the Genesis creation narrative.

In Genesis 1:26 and 1:28, God tells humanity to "radah" over the earth: the fish in the sea, the birds in the air, the animals, the earth itself, and all living things.

The word "radah" is often translated as "have dominion over" or "rule over," but I believe "be responsible for" better captures its intent. As Andrew Basden explains:

"Our radah of creation is not to be with harshness, cruelty, or selfishness. It is not for our sake, but for the sake of creation itself. We are to heal what is sick, bind up what is injured, and care for creation as shepherds—not destroyers or mere consumers, but compassionate caretakers who develop, refine, and beautify creation for its own sake."

This perspective reminds us that environmental wellness is not optional; it is integral to our purpose as stewards of creation.

"You will bless everyone who respects and obeys you, whether they are important people or not. But you will destroy all those people who destroy the earth."

REVELATION 11:18

Environmental wellness calls us to deepen our relationship with creation. The outdoors is a sanctuary where we can connect with something larger than ourselves.

As we cultivate our physical and environmental wellness, let us craft experiences and encounters with creation that nurture our bodies, minds, and spirits. Whether planting trees, sitting under their shade, or walking the paths of wild places, may we honor the earth as both gift and responsibility.

"It is better to go skiing and think of God, than to go to church and think of sport."

FRIDTJOF NANSEN

CREATION ENCOUNTERS

I have walked well over 4,782 miles with my son Aram, exploring the wilderness of life and nature—both backcountry and front country. His first hike at age four was a climb in the White Mountains of New Hampshire. During his elementary and middle school years, I'd occasionally pull him out of class early to spend the rest of the day discovering the trails of nearby state parks. Those single-day adventures evolved into overnight hiking and camping trips during high school. By college, we were hiking across Scotland, trekking through desert canyonlands, climbing snow-covered Adirondack peaks, and wandering urban alleyways and landscapes.

As Aram puts it, "We continue to build the muscles of connection with wild nature, leaning into our relationship with earth through attention and action."

This rhythm of regularly encountering nature has become central to our wellness and vitality. We have lived with the will and belief that regular proximity with nature is a vital rhythm for wellness and being fully alive. Together, we've carved out space and pace to create moments of connection with wild places—encounters that feed and sustain our souls.

FOUR LEVELS OF NATURE ENCOUNTERS

Let me suggest four ways to engage with nature's rhythms and intersections, whether in the backcountry or the front country. Since these encounters feed the heart, soul, and mind, I like to use food on the trail analogies to describe them:

1. Taste or Sip

A brief, casual moment with nature. Step away from your task, go outside, and look around, listen, and breathe deeply. Offer a prayer of gratitude or a psalm of wonder. These small, fleeting encounters can be woven into your daily routine—a sip of creation's goodness.

On the trail, it's that moment when you pause for a sip of water or a quick nibble of jerky or an energy bar from your pocket.

2. Snack

An intentional pause—a little more time carved out to indulge in the outdoors. It might last fourteen minutes, fifty-seven minutes, or somewhere in between. This is an opportunity to reflect and reconnect. You could explore a wooded area, wander through a park, or stroll along an alleyway, sidewalk, or neighborhood path.

Take time to walk, sit, or lie on your back—intentionally creating space to slow down and tune in to nature.

As Aram says, "Connect with as much nature as you can muster." And as John Muir reminds us, "It is spending time in the half-wild parks and gardens of town."

Whatever the environment or posture, the essence is the same: getting outside to engage with creation. On the trail, it might look like a mid-morning or mid-afternoon break: setting down your pack, enjoying a handful of trail mix, some cheese, or jerky, and maybe even brewing a cup of tea or coffee.

3. Meal

A dedicated day or two in the woods or on the water. This is an extended overnight getaway from routine to refresh your mind, body, and spirit. A space and pace to reignite a deeper connection with the earth a few times a year.

On the trail, it's gathering at a campsite to share a slow, deliberate meal—unpacking supplies, preparing food, winding down with conversations and reflecting on the day's journey together.

4. Feast

A deeper, extended dive into nature—a wilderness adventure or a pilgrimage. This is a deliberate step away from routine and a step into creation, requiring both sacrifice and thoughtful preparation. These encounters vary in immersion and duration, offering opportunities for meaningful connection with the natural world. It might be seasonal, annual, or even a once-in-a-lifetime experience.

On the trail, this is a last-night meal of food and drink that has been packed and carried to celebrate the journey with gratitude and reflection. We gather to share stories and savor the encounters—both inward and outward—of the preceding days.

REFLECTION QUESTIONS

What am I doing now to lean into nature with my body, brain, and breath?

What plans can I set to build the muscles of my relationship with creation?

A WANDER AND A WONDER EXPERIENCE

Visit a farmer's market. Touch, smell, listen, see, talk, dirt, seed, grow, taste. Immerse yourself in the experience: Touch the produce, smell the herbs, listen to the sounds, and take in the colors and textures of the season's bounty. Purchase ingredients for a meal you'll prepare from scratch. Share the experience and the meal with others.

Around the table, reflect and wonder together...
- wonder about parables Jesus told about soil and growth and plants and meals.

- wonder about bread and wine,communion, shared meals and community.

- wonder about gardens and stories of redemption and restoration and what they might invite you into...

LECTIO DIVINA PRACTICE

Lying in a meadow green, Dangling legs in a mountain stream From a limb we could jump right in, Again and again and again and again

RAY LAMONTAGNE, "LONG WAY HOME"

Find Ray LaMontagne's song, "Long Way Home." (Seek out the "Official Music Video" version.) Listen to it several times. Let the words, music and spirit percolate in your heart and mind. Walk with it. Sit with it. Practice some Lectio Divina with it.

Stepping Into Pilgrimage... A Practical Guide

Step out
Not just to move but to be moved.
Step out with a thought, a question, a song, a poem
Let curiosity guide your pace
Feel Listen Notice
Breathe
Pause
Measure moments not miles
Step out
See what the path reveals

I'm guessing you have caught the concept that pilgrimage is more than a journey to faraway places—it's an intentional movement of body, mind, and spirit. Whether a short stroll through your neighborhood, a sauntering afternoon hike through a nearby park, or a multi-day trek into the wilderness, pilgrimage invites us to move through the world with awareness, curiosity, and openness to transformation. Here are some simple movements and practical hints for your own pilgrimage experiences. This is not a comprehensive guide but rather a spark for exploration as I invite you to step onto the path with a sense of engagement, discovery, and reflection.

1. **Step Out...Prepare with Purpose:** Whether stepping into front-country wild (urban sidewalks and alleyways) or backcountry wild (desert or forest paths), the first step marks a shift. You leave behind routine and step into the unknown, embracing curiosity, openness, and the possibility of transformation. Take a moment to mark your beginning. Consider a word, a question, a poem, or a prayer—something to carry with you as you walk. What draws you to this walk? Is it reflection, renewal, or simply curiosity? Set an intention, even if it's just "to notice."

2. **Saunter...Pace & Presence:** Pilgrimage is not about speed or distance; it is about presence. Know your route, but allow space for curiosity. Some of the best discoveries are unplanned. Walk with a rhythm that allows you to listen for the whispers of wisdom from the elements around you. Move with a balance of silence and conversation, effort and rest, solitude and communion. Saunter at a gentle pace. Slow down enough to notice. Pause. Look around. Soak in the moment. Jot down thoughts. Let curiosity, not efficiency, set your stride. Embrace some silence. Consider silencing your phone or putting it in wilderness mode (some phones call it airplane mode). Find a stump, a bench, a rock and sit to observe and soak in the world around you. And if the moment is right, exert yourself with a challenging pace. And please, please, please honor and respect the space you walk. Whether front country urban or backcountry wilderness, be mindful of the land, the people and the stories along the way.

3. **Return...With Reflection:** A pilgrimage does not end when you leave the experience. An early morning stroll on city sidewalks, an afternoon snowshoe hike, a multi-day hike along ancient paths, the experience lingers and shapes—in memory, in perspective shifts, in subtle changes to how you engage the world. As you finish, take moments to ponder...What did you notice?

What surprised you? What will you carry forward into daily life?

4. **Walk Freely...Pack Right, Pack Light:** Essentials vary by journey, but water, a snack, a small notebook, and weather-appropriate clothing and footwear are good starting points.

For short walks and hikes consider...
- sturdy, comfortable footwear.
- clothing..Avoid cotton (especially jeans) in favor of breathable, moisture-wicking layers. Be ready for changing weather.
- water bottle (with water in it)
- snacks
- sun protection
- bug repellent
- pencil and paper
- a small first aid kit with any personal emergency medications
- map and compass

For overnight or multi-day hikes research...
- the physical nature of the place: terrain, climate, and challenges
- necessary gear: lightweight backpacking essentials, appropriate footwear, clothing, shelter, food, hydration
- reliable resources: local trail associations, national park websites, and gear recommendations from experienced hikers

Pilgrimage, whether an hour or a month long—step out, move through, and return changed. The streets and trails await.

Earth Campsite

G reat walk...you finished the Earth Element. Now imagine yourself finishing this section of the walk and setting up camp: your kitchen, your sleeping nook, your journaling/reading/yoga space...basically the campsite that gets on the cover of Backpacker Magazine.

After each of the four Elements there will be an opportunity to sit and reflect on a conversation around the kitchen circle. Just an extra wee bonus pulled out of the pack...perhaps a dark chocolate bar, perhaps a small bottle of Scotch. A chance to sit back, look into a star filled sky, tell stories, laugh, confess, and share life. Here is the campsite for the Earth Element...and yes, rather appropriate, I guess.

EARTH CAMPSITE MOMENT: A TASTE OF HOME

I often tell people I hike to camp and eat. There's few things like the joy and satisfaction of finding a great campsite—the reward of the walk. For me, a campsite is a taste of heaven on the way home: a place of smiles, tears, silence, filling, hope, understanding, grace, rest, nurture, and sustenance.

Whether it's a physical campsite or a metaphorical one, reflect on your own "campsite moments"—those spaces and places where you significantly connect with self, others, life.

A campsite moment...

A campsite companion...

A campsite taste...

A campsite lesson...

A campsite feeling...

EARTH CAMPSITE...REFLECTIONS, WONDERINGS, PONDERINGS, DOODLINGS

Feet planted in the soil, eyes lifted to the stars. As I explore the depths, textures, and layers of being human—grounded in physical presence and awareness—what emerges?

What makes my heart come **ALIVE?**

What makes my soul **SING?**

What moves my spirit to **DANCE?**

WATER

LECTIO DIVINA PRACTICE

I come into the presence of still water. And I feel above me the day-blind stars waiting with their light. For a time I rest in the grace of the world, and am free.

WENDELL BERRY

Find Wendell Berry's poem, "The Peace of Wild Things." Read it a few times. Let the words and spirit of it percolate in your heart and mind. Walk with it. Sit with it. Practice some Lectio Divina with it.

Was the Water Squishy?

"At about four o'clock in the morning, Jesus came toward them walking on the water."

MATTHEW 14:26

"Whoever drinks the water I give them will never thirst. Indeed, the water I give them will become in them a spring of water welling up to eternal life."

JOHN 4:14

"Six stoneware water pots were there, used by the Jews for ritual washings. Each held twenty to thirty gallons. Jesus ordered the servants, 'Fill the pots with water.' And they filled them to the brim."

JOHN 2:6–7

Jesus was at home walking dirt paths and working with his hands. He also seemed quite comfortable around water—whether drinking it, traveling across it, or according to legend even strolling on it. There's so much to wonder and imagine about in Jesus' encounters with water.

I invite you to read these stories—Matthew 14:22-33, John 4:5-30, and John 2:1-11—and wonder with me. A reminder: Don't read them like a scholar seeking answers. Instead, approach them with curiosity and imagination, like a child hearing a story for the first time. And have fun.

Personally, I like reading these encounters from The Message, a paraphrase of the Bible in "contemporary" English. Its simplicity and clarity works for me. Use whatever version works for you—and don't force it.

WONDERING WITH WATER

Did Jesus' feet get wet when he walked on water? Did it feel firm like a wood floor, or soft and squishy? What sound did his footsteps make?

What went through the Samaritan woman's mind when she saw Jesus sitting alone at the well? Was she scared, nervous, curious, or apprehensive?

Did she see him as a potential suitor, considering her complicated history with relationships?

How did the disciples react when they found Jesus talking with her? Surprise, disapproval, curiosity, or unease?

Why did she leave her water jug behind when she ran back to the town?

How did John find out what was said in the conversation? Did he ask Jesus or the lady or was there someone else around who was listening in?

When Jesus asked her for a drink did he have specific intentional plans of guiding a conversation that would later be recorded in the Gospel of John or was he just thirsty?

Did he know or hope she would push back and respond with a question or two of her own rather than giving him the water?

Was the whole encounter an unplanned, unscripted, spontaneous, organic response to life?

Why did she leave her water jug behind when she ran back to the town?

And what about the wedding in Cana?

How did Jesus' mother feel when he pushed back on her request? Hurt, disappointed, or just feisty?

Did Mary give him that unmistakable mom look that said, "You may be the Son of Jehovah, but you're still my son. Now do what I asked,"?

What were the servants thinking as they filled the jars? Did they sense this was about meeting a need, not putting on a show?

Was the food still being eaten or had the celebration moved into the dance and drink stage?

What were his dance moves like, especially with his 4-year-old niece?

There's something deeply human and profoundly sacred in these stories. The more I sit with them, the more I wonder:

Was Jesus' conversation at the well a spontaneous, organic moment? Or did he know exactly where it would lead?

Did he plan to turn water into wine, or was it simply a compassionate response to what was happening?

THE GIFT OF WATER

Water makes up about **75% of the earth's surface** and **55–65% of the human body.** Basically, all the systems of the human body need water to work, and life on earth pretty much depends on water. It is essential for physical survival, yet it holds a deeper significance for the mind, body, and spirit.

Think about it: Homes with a water view cost significantly more than similar structures without. Hotel rooms with an ocean view are more expensive than the same rooms on the other side of the hotel. Why? Is it because water has a measurable, positive effect on our mental and emotional well-being? Is it because the sights, sounds,

and touches of water bring soothing to the human spirit? Studies suggest that simply being near water can:
- Lower stress and anxiety
- Lower risk of premature death
- Reduce heart rates and risk of obesity
- Improve mental clarity and emotional balance

In *Blue Mind: The Surprising Science That Shows How Being Near, In, On, or Under Water Can Make You Happier, Healthier, More Connected, and Better at What You Do*, marine biologist Wallace J. Nichols explores the profound connection between water and well-being. I encourage you to add it to your reading list.

Nichols' ideas have me imagining heaven not with streets of gold, but with houses by the water.

But for now here are some water thoughts to wander and wonder with...

bpibanti nadyaḥ svayameva nāmbhaḥ
svayaṃ na khādanti phalāni vṛkṣāḥ
nādanti sasyaṃ khalu vārivāhāḥ
paropakārāya satāṃ vibhūtayaḥ

Just as the rivers do not drink their own water but flow for others' benefit, just as fruit-bearing trees do not eat their own fruit but bear it for others, and just as clouds do not drink their own rain but shower it down on others, so saintly devotees live simply for others.

SANSKRIT PROVERB

"I hate all those weathermen, too, who tell you that rain is bad weather. There is no such thing as bad weather, just the

wrong clothing, so get yourself a raincoat and live a little."

BILLY CONNOLLY

"If you want to build a ship, don't drum up the men to gather wood, divide the work, and give orders. Instead, teach them to yearn for the vast and endless sea."

ANTOINE DE SAINT-EXUPÉRY

"I believe that water is the closest thing to a god we have here on Earth. We are in awe of its power and majestic beauty. We are drawn to it as if it's a magical, healing force. We gestate in water, are made of water, and need to drink water to live. We are living in water."

ALEX Z. MOORES, LIVING IN WATER

"Some people love the ocean. Some people fear it. I love it, hate it, fear it, respect it, cherish it, loathe it, and frequently curse it. It brings out the best in me and sometimes the worst."

ROZ SAVAGE

"Dripping water hollows out stone, not through force but through persistence"

PUBLIUS OVIDIUS NASO

"Until justice rolls down like water and righteousness like a mighty stream."

MARTIN LUTHER KING, JR.

"Live in the sunshine, swim the sea, and drink the wild air."

RALPH WALDO EMERSON

"When the wells dry, we know the worth of water"

BEN FRANKLIN

"My therapist set half a glass of water in front of me. He asked if I was an optimist or a pessimist. So, I drank the water and told him I was a problem solver."

UNKNOWN

REFLECTIONS

Take some time to reflect on these questions:

What is my relationship with water?

What are some of my favorite water memories?

How do I feel—deep in my being—when I am near an ocean, river, stream, lake, or waterfall? What do my senses notice?

What does it mean to me to be in the presence of still waters?

THIRST AND LIVING WATER

When have I been thirsty, really really thirsty? Deer panting for the water, aching for springs of living water in the desert thirsty? What was it like to finally get a drink? With that memory guiding my reflection...

What does that kind of thirst invite me to consider about my life?

Where do I see thirst—for justice, healing, or restoration—in the world around me?

How might I respond?

Mental Wellness

This part of the path might feel like a switchback or a meander that suddenly veered off course. We were just reflecting on water and thirst, so how did we end up talking about mental wellness?

Let's go back to what you just considered:

What do you feel deep in your being when you are in the presence of an ocean, river, stream, lake, or waterfall?

How do your senses respond—sight, sound, touch, even taste or smell?

I'm guessing those reflections stirred deep sighs of peace, connection, and well-being. And that's where water ties into mental wellness.

WHAT IS MENTAL WELLNESS?

Mental wellness is about much more than our IQ score, ability to take tests, and think cognitively. It's also about the ways we use our mind to communicate, to watch a movie or listen to a song, to meditate, to handle the flow of life. It's a dynamic, active process shaping how we:

- Think and feel
- Handle emotions
- Relate to others
- Navigate daily life

The Global Wellness Institute defines mental wellness as: "An internal resource that helps us think, feel, connect, and function; it is an active process that helps us build resilience, grow, and flourish."

In essence, mental wellness allows us to think, feel, and act in ways that positively influence our lives. It informs:

- How we feel about ourselves
- How we manage relationships
- How we approach life's challenges

I once heard it said, "Being mentally well means my mind is functioning in my best interest." I believe the functioning in my best interest is a "best interest" that isn't about selfishness but is about fostering selflessness, leading to compassion rather than callousness toward others.

SINGING IN THE RAIN: AN EXERCISE IN MENTAL WELLNESS

Rain is a gift. Rain invites us to step out of routine, embrace the unexpected, and connect with a world that is alive and flourishing. It reminds us that life isn't always about sunny skies, but there's beauty and nourishment in the storm. Rain can renew the earth—and us—if we let it.

One of my favorite mental wellness practices is taking intentional, playful, and contemplative walks in the rain.

HERE'S WHAT I LOVE ABOUT IT

Playfulness: Jumping in puddles, splashing, and giggling awaken a childlike joy that's too often buried under the weight of daily life.

Contemplation: Listening to the rhythm of falling raindrops and reflecting on the life being nurtured by water creates space for mindfulness and peace.

REFLECTIONS ON RAIN

Take some moments to consider:

What do I like about rainy days?

What feels different—in a good way—when I'm outside in the rain?

What might I notice if I truly listen to the rain as it nourishes the earth and invites play?

Could I ask friends or family to help me create a list of all the things to love about rainy days?

How might I embrace walking, singing, or simply being in the rain?

AND PUDDLE JUMP...

Mental wellness, like rain, nourishes us when we let it. It's about embracing the unexpected, finding joy in simplicity, and allowing ourselves to feel deeply. Whether it's walking in the rain, reflecting by still waters, or connecting with others, these practices build resilience and bring life to our minds, hearts, and spirits.

So the next time the clouds gather and the rain begins to fall, don't just stay inside. Grab a raincoat—or leave it behind—and head out to sing, play, reflect, and let the rain refresh your body, mind, and spirit. And of course I recommend a good hearty splash jump into a puddle while shouting, "ALIVE!!!"

A Posture of Questions, Listening, and Conversation

I'm intrigued by the mental wellness dynamic of Jesus' life. While countless books offer interpretations and beliefs about him, the historical records are sparse. Most of what we know comes from the Bible—primarily the Gospels, a bit from Acts, and letters from Paul and others. Beyond these, there are brief mentions by historians like Josephus, Tacitus, Pliny, and Suetonius.

So when Luke writes that Jesus grew mentally and physically during childhood, **a lot is left to imagination and curiosity.**

- How did he approach learning?
- Did he already know it all?
- Did he struggle with calculus and physics, or did he just smile and think, *I kind of helped invent this stuff?*
- Would he have crushed it on *Jeopardy!* without any practice or study?

Whatever the "grew in mind" part looked like, I love the glimpses we get into this dynamic of his life. For instance, there's the story of 12-year-old Jesus going missing for three days. His parents found him in the temple courts, sitting among the teachers, **listening to them and asking them questions.** Those who heard him were amazed at his understanding and his answers (Luke 2:46–47). It's the "listening and asking questions" that sparks my imagination. His understanding was clearly remarkable, but what draws me is his curiosity and his willingness to listen and engage. **Imagine the depth of those conversations.**

A MIND OPEN TO CONVERSATION

This spirit of curiosity and attentiveness shows up again and again in his life:

- His nighttime conversation with Nicodemus (John 3)
- His dialogue with the Samaritan woman at the well (John 4)
- The countless encounters where he connected deeply with those around him

Jesus wasn't about delivering lectures or preaching down to people. Instead, he invited them into conversations that opened new ways of thinking and being. His approach wasn't deductive—simply giving answers—but inductive, sparking curiosity and reflection. Through parables, imagery, and lived examples, he created space for people to wrestle, reflect, and come to their own conclusions.

Here's what I imagine: After Jesus told a parable or performed a healing, what happened next?

- What kinds of questions did people ask each other?
- How did they wrestle with what they had seen or heard?
- What insights emerged as they processed together?

Imagine the conversations after moments like these:

- Jesus touching a leper (Mark 1:40–45)
- Healing on the Sabbath (Mark 3:1–6; Luke 13:10–17; John 9:1–16)
- Posture towards the woman who anointed him with tears and perfume (Luke 7:36–50)
- Refusing to condemn the woman caught in adultery (John 7:53–8:11)

I believe the richest insights came not just from the stories themselves but from the conversations that followed—the shared pondering, wondering, and discovery among those who were there.

The Practice of Asking Questions and Listening

Our culture often values quick answers, convenience, and certainty. Why wrestle with questions when we can demand answers from someone eager to provide them? Why seek at all when apathy and indifference are an option?

In contrast, Jesus modeled a way of living that embraces curiosity, questions, and deep listening. His life invites us to wrestle, seek, and converse—not in isolation but in community. Faith isn't just an individual pursuit or a personal pass into heaven. Faith grows in relationships, through shared questions and collaborative discoveries.

At its heart, Jesus' way of living was an invitation to **put love where love is not**—to lean into the work of healing, redemption, and love in a world that deeply needs it.

"Where there is no love, put love, and you will find love"
ST. JOHN OF THE CROSS, SPANISH MYSTIC AND SAINT

CONVERSATIONS THAT SHAPE US

I've heard it said that a conversion is any shift of belief that significantly alters the course of a life. Most significant conversions are rooted in conversations—conversations shaped by listening, questions, and mutual respect. Jesus valued people's minds, encouraging them to wrestle and wonder without coercion or manipulation. In doing so, he nurtured and affirmed their mental wellness.

REFLECTION PROMPTS

What spaces am I creating for conversations soaked in questions and listening?

A recent conversation that challenged me...

A conversation that shaped me...

A couple of questions I'd like to explore with friends—or with a guide...

Navigating the Currents and Waves

For me, water has often been a source of peace, clarity, and inspiration. The sound, sight, and presence of it brings a balance of comfort and invigoration. A few years ago, I spent a week paddling the Wisconsin River with my son and a couple of friends. That adventure was one of those spaces where life and nature converged to shape and teach.

Here's a portion of Aram's journal from that journey:

"I was paddling on the Wisconsin River with my dad and a couple of other hearty souls. We were paddling downstream into a fierce wind that whipped up waves that all but reversed the current. Cold rain stung our eyes. This was the stuff of the tohu va bohu—the chaos of the wilderness—that preceded creation in the origin myth of the Hebrew Bible.

I was in the stern of one of our two canoes, responsible for keeping the boat rightly oriented to the wind and waves. A touch too much in one direction and the wind would catch the bow, twisting us broadside to the waves. My mind was empty of all but the task of holding this balance. I say 'mind,' but I had no time between gusts for conscious calculation. My whole body—my whole sensory self—partook in the task.

And for all its ferocity, the wind was not a foe, nor the current, nor the waves. They were companions in this play of balance. Each gust on my cheek informed the lean of my torso, the way my wrists angled the blade of the paddle in the water, the muscle I put into each stroke, or my restrained pause between gusts...

After the storm calmed enough for us to make some conscious calculations, we captained our canoes to the lee side of an island on the Wisconsin River. We set up camp on the sandy beach, boiled tortellini, and mixed it with pesto, then propped ourselves up against boulders to watch the colors of that day's sunset bounce on the remaining waves and on our own awed faces...

The natural will of the world leans toward regeneration and invites us to lean in the same direction, contributing as members of this vast, earth-sized community of redemption and renewal."

LEANING TOWARD RENEWAL

How does Aram's closing thought—leaning toward regeneration, redemption, and renewal—settle in your mind? For me, it feels like a compass pointing toward something bigger than ourselves. It reminds me of a similar idea captured in this quote: "The purpose of life is not to be happy. It is to be useful, to be honorable, to be compassionate, to have it make some difference that you have lived and lived well."

If you Google this quote, it's often attributed to Ralph Waldo Emerson. Some sources, however, suggest Leo Rosten deserves the credit. Perhaps this ambiguity reminds us that the quest for truth isn't usually straightforward. It requires diligence, curiosity, and sometimes a little Google mixed with a lot of wonder.

But no matter who said it first, the thought itself is worthy of exploration.

To live this way—to be useful, honorable, and compassionate—requires navigating challenging waters. Life's currents, winds, and waves often try to push us off course or capsize us. At times, we need to lay the paddle across our laps and see where the current carries us. Other times, we must paddle fiercely, fighting the current like crazy.

Paddling reminds us of the balance required in life—of the need to lean toward something greater than ourselves. Whether we're riding the waves or resting on calm waters, we are part of a vast, interconnected community. To contribute to it is to make a difference.

REFLECTIONS FROM THE RIVER AND NAVIGATING LIFE'S CURRENTS

What does regeneration, redemption, and renewal look like to me?

What does it mean to be useful, honorable, and compassionate?

How can I make a difference and live well?

What currents are carrying me toward being a vessel of regeneration, a participant in renewal and redemption?

What currents are trying to pull me away from that?

How can I keep my mind curious, alert, and sharpened to the spaces and paces I'm navigating?

MORE WATERS TO EXPLORE

What, where, when, how, and why do I want to explore, pushing away from the shores where I'm harbored?

What am I afraid of?

What should I be afraid of?

How can I weave renewal into my intimate, incarnate encounters with the world and all its wildness?

What does it mean for me to be useful, to be honorable, to be compassionate?

To make a difference and to live well?

LECTIO DIVINA PRACTICE

I've come a long, long road, but still have some miles to go I've got a wide, wide river to cross

LEVON HELM, "WIDE RIVER TO CROSS"

Find The White Horse Guitar Club's version of the song, "Wide River To Cross." Listen to it and watch it a few times. Let the words, the music, and the spirit of it percolate in your heart and mind. Paddle with it. Sit with it. Practice some Lectio Divina with it.

Vocational Wellness

"Vocation is the place where our deep gladness meets the world's deep need."

FREDERICK BUECHNER

"Our job in life is not to shape ourselves into some ideal we imagine we ought to be, but to find out who we already are and become it."

STEVEN PRESSFIELD, THE WAR OF ART

"Today I understand vocation quite differently—not as a goal to be achieved, but as a gift to be received. Discovering vocation does not mean scrambling toward some prize just beyond my reach, but accepting the treasure of true self I already possess. Vocation does not come from a voice 'out there' calling me to become something I am not. It comes from a voice 'in here' calling me to be the person I was born to be."

PARKER PALMER, LET YOUR LIFE SPEAK

TUESDAYS WITH NAPKIN

When Aram was in middle school, I would drive him to school on Tuesday mornings. Our ritual included breakfast at McDonald's, where we'd talk about life. Often, I'd sketch or doodle a simple concept on a napkin for us to ponder.

One Tuesday, he asked me what he should do with his life—both now and in the future. I drew a foot with an exaggeratedly large big toe and told him to follow his **TOE**.

I'll never forget the quizzical look on his face—probably similar to yours right now. TOE? It stands for:

- **Talents:** What are you good at?
- **Opportunities:** What doors are opening for you?
- **Enthusiasms**: What ignites your passion?

Aram went on to become an outstanding science student, earning awards and scholarships throughout high school. His grandfather hoped he would become a doctor—he had the talent and opportunities to do so, and his relational skills would have made him an excellent one. But his enthusiasm wasn't there. He didn't want to invest his life in something he wasn't passionate about.

Now, many years after that napkin Tuesday, he is a prophet, pilgrim, provocator, poet, and practitioner in the field of wilderness and spiritual care—and fully *alive*! (Check out confluenceformation. com or arammitchell.com for more about his journey.)

For myself, I'm enthusiastic about hockey and singing in a blues band. I regularly do both, and I'm fairly decent at them. But enthusiasm alone wasn't enough to make either my vocation. I recognized early on that I lacked the talent and opportunities to be a professional hockey player.

WHAT IS VOCATIONAL WELLNESS?

Vocational wellness is about finding purpose, satisfaction, and fulfillment in our work while maintaining balance in our lives. It's about making a positive impact in the places where we work, study, volunteer, and live.

It involves discovering, blending, and expressing our talents, passions, values, interests, opportunities, hobbies, and relationships. It's about walking the path where your unique footprint in the world meets its greatest needs.

When stepping onto this path, it helps to explore with curiosity the major areas of need in the world—physical, relational, societal, personal, environmental, and spiritual—and to layer in the perspectives shaped by your own life experience.

THREE STARTING POINTS FOR EXPLORING VOCATION

When I reflect on how I approach vocational wellness—seeking purpose, maintaining balance, and making a positive impact—I start with three foundational steps:

1. **I am a creation, not the Creator.**
   My comprehension is limited, but it is seeded with creativity, imagination, and a unique mix of gifts, passions, and values.
2. **I am a blend of contradictions.**
   I am a scofflaw, skeptic, seeker, sinner, and saint. I have the capacity for both good and evil, selfishness and selflessness. What I comprehend often gets tangled in the tension between serving the world and serving my self-interests.
3. **I am shaped by my cultural context.**
   I am a white Canadian male and currently living in Indiana. My heritage, family, and upbringing influence my values, assumptions, and approaches. To grow, I must intentionally step outside this context and engage with other perspectives and cultural values with an open heart and mind. I step outside and explore by listening, travelling, reading engaging with open mind, heart and spirit out of my context or comfort spaces.

THE CONTINUOUS JOURNEY OF
VOCATIONAL WELLNESS

The pursuit of vocational wellness is a dynamic, ongoing process. It invites consistent learning, skill development, and reflection on why and how we work, play, serve, and love—both ourselves and our neighbors.

As Emily Esfahani Smith writes, vocational wellness is as much about perception as it is about the work itself:

"It is about my perception, attitude, outlook, and reaction to the work I take part in. Ambition, desire for satisfaction, and yearning for advancement vary from person to person; each is on their own path with their own set of vocational wellness goals.

A vocationally well person selects an occupation that utilizes their gifts, strengths, and skills and aligns with their interests and values. A vocationally well person strives to balance work and non-work obligations and activities, including learning how to say 'no' to maintain that balance."

IT'S WORTH ASKING

Parker Palmer writes, "When we love what we do, we bring love—not only to it, but to everyone affected by it."

How does your vocation or desired vocation reflect love?

What gifts, passions, and perspectives are you offering to the world?

EXPLORE THE WATERS...VALUES, SKILLS, AND MORE

Imagine yourself—or better yet, actually do it—in a canoe, kayak, or sailboat on a favorite body of water: a river, lake, or creek. You're paddling, or perhaps intentionally drifting with the currents, casting your line in a dance with the water. Spend some time, over spans of time, wandering and wondering with these thoughts and questions as your companions.

CORE VALUES

What are core values, and why are they meaningful?

Maps, trail markers, and landmarks are essential for guiding me, especially when on a new hike or paddling adventure. Core values serve a similar purpose: They are the beliefs, principles, and perspectives that guide and shape our behaviors as we navigate life. They influence our actions, decisions, and beliefs. They shape what we stand for—and what we live for.

Here is a sampling and smattering and scattering of words that capture core values. Read through them quickly at first. I know it is a like a long, long, long run-on sentence that way, but you can do it. Let them rush through your head and heart like a fast flowing river or mountain stream.

Achievement, adventurous, advocate for the underdog, animal rights, arts, authentic, autonomy, beauty, charitable, civil disobedience, committed, common sense, community development, collaborative, community, compassionate, competitive, concerned for others, consistent, courageous, craftsmanship, creativity, curiosity, dependable, dominant, education, enthusiastic, environmentalism, equality, ethical, fairness, faith, fame, family, fearless, fitness, freedom, friendship, good humor, generosity, happiness, honesty, honorable, human rights, individual liberties, influence, joy, justice, kindness,

knowledge, laughter, leadership, love, loyalty, legacy, mercy, nurturing, open-mindedness, patriotic, peace, perseverance, pleasure, popularity, positivity, purpose, reliability, religion, reputation, respect, rule of law, security, servanthood, social justice, spirituality, stability, success, tolerance, transparency, trust, virtue, wealth, wisdom.

Now revisit that long, long long run on sentence. Slower this time, pausing between each. Perhaps as if you were sitting in a boat on a lake, soaking in your surroundings, a hand in the water, feeling it slowly flow through your fingers. Or casting a fishing line in the waters, patiently watching and waiting for a nibble on the line.

Let each word linger in the currents.

What values jumped out of the water and invited me to pause and pay attention?

What comes to mind or heart as I reflect on each one?

Is this value a strength I already live by?

Is it a guide that shapes my life?

Is it a challenge to how I do life?

Is it a value I've neglected but feel stirred to nurture?

VOCATIONAL SKILLS.

By definition: the skill or set of skills that help a person get and grow in a job. Surgeons, musicians, mechanics, software designers, hairdressers, hockey players, and plumbers are examples of vocations that require their own set of unique skills. But there are also **transferable skills**—general qualities valuable across vocations. Here is a sampling and smattering and scattering of vocational skills...you know, the types of things employers look for. Again, first read through once quickly, letting them move through your head and heart like that fast flowing river or mountain stream.

Confidence, research, analysis, balance, teamwork, focus, critical thinking, emotional intelligence, organization, persuasiveness, efficiency, collaboration, accountability, creativity, teachability, cross-cultural understanding, technology, self-direction, innovation, flexibility, productivity, reflection, responsibility, attention to detail, responsiveness.

Approach them in a similar way that you did with the vocational values. Do any of the skills invite you to pause and sit on the bank for a bit?

Now, return to the list—slowly. Sit again in the boat, hand trailing in the currents, or casting your fishing line with patience.

Let each skill linger.

Is it a strength I rely on?

A weakness I'd like to improve?

A challenge I feel ready to take on?

WHAT WATERS AM I EXPLORING: A DEEPENING REFLECTION...EXPLORING VALUES AND SKILLS

What values significantly influence how I live out my place in the world?

What values are calling for more attention or involvement in my life?

Am I looking at my values through a lens of generosity and compassion—or through the lens of wanting to look good to others and feel good about myself?

What are my natural talents?

What are my passions?

What are my interests?

What are my commitments? (Remember: Interests may come and go, but commitments stick.)

What are my strengths?

What are my weaknesses?

What experiences have shaped me?

What knowledge do I bring to the table?

What stirs my compassion?

What kind of work makes me feel alive?

LECTIO DIVINA PRACTICE

"The people I love the best jump into work head first without dallying in the shallows and swim off with sure strokes almost out of sight."

MARGE PIERCY

Find Piercy's full poem, "To Be of Use." Read it a few times. Let its words percolate in your heart and mind. Walk with it. Sit with it. Practice Lectio Divina with it, letting its spirit guide your thoughts and dreams about values, skills, and vocational wellness.

Backhand Shot... Learning Something New

I play ball hockey in a couple of leagues, and some players seem like they were born to stick handle, shoot, pass, and defend. Their moves are effortless, as if they were hardwired for the game. They waste no time or energy thinking about the next move—they just perform.

For me, it has been a lifetime of learning. Now, in my seventh decade of playing, many of the essential skills feel like second nature. But occasionally, a new skill or approach grabs my attention, and I realize that if I want to be a better player, I need to take the time to learn it.

When I was eight or nine years old, I watched a Toronto Maple Leafs game on *Hockey Night in Canada*. Dave Keon, my favorite player, scored two goals that night—both with a backhand shot. I'd never given much thought to backhand shooting before, but seeing my hero pull it off twice on national TV changed everything. I wanted to be just like him, so I started practicing backhand shots day after day, week after week.

Over time, without realizing it, I moved through the four stages of the conscious competence matrix, a model that explains how we learn and acquire new skills. Decades later, a backhand shot has become second nature—I can do it without a second thought. While mastering this skill wasn't essential to my career or education, it has been a rewarding and fun part of my life.

Not all learning journeys have gone as smoothly. A few years after honing my backhand, I set my sights on becoming the next great blues or rock guitarist. That dream, however, was short-lived. I remained stuck between stages 1 and 2 because, truthfully, I preferred playing hockey over practicing guitar. In my imagination and dreams, I did stick with it—if only!

These two experiences—the backhand shot and the stalled guitar dream—illustrate the four stages of the conscious competence matrix. So, take a look at these four stages, and then spend some time pondering...

FOUR STAGES OF LEARNING

1. Unconscious Incompetence – Ignorance

"I don't know what I don't know."

At this stage, we are unaware of a skill or our lack of proficiency in it. We don't know what we're missing, and in our ignorance, we might even deny the importance of learning it—until something sparks our curiosity or recognition of a need.

When I was nine, I didn't even think about backhand shots until I saw Dave Keon score those two goals. Similarly, there was a time when I didn't realize how much I didn't know about playing guitar— or about how much practice it would take to become proficient. Ignorance can feel blissful—until we realize what we're missing.

2. Conscious Incompetence – Awareness

"I realize what I don't know."

Here, we become aware of the skill we lack. We recognize it's something we need, want, or should be able to do. While we're far from proficient, this is where learning begins. Mistakes are inevitable, but they are part of the process as we explore and practice the new skill.

At this stage, I spent hours fumbling with backhand shots—missing the net more times than I can count. And when it came to guitar, I started to recognize just how much I didn't know. The difference? I stuck with practicing my backhand, but I avoided practicing guitar. Progress requires perseverance, and my love for hockey outweighed my commitment to learning music.

3. Conscious Competence - Learning

"I can do it, but I have to think about it."

Through practice and consistent effort, we start to develop the skill. At this stage, we can perform it, but it still requires concentration and effort.

Eventually, my backhand shot started landing in the net—but only if I focused on my hand placement and follow-through. Guitar, on the other hand, never made it to this stage. In my imagination, I could play "Stairway to Heaven," but in reality, I rarely picked up the guitar.

4. Unconscious Competence - Mastery

"I just do it—it's second nature."

At this stage, we've mastered the skill. It feels natural, as if it's always been a part of us. We don't need to consciously think about it anymore; we simply know and do.

Now, I can take a backhand shot in the middle of a fast-paced hockey game without a second thought—it just happens. Guitar, however, stayed a dream. And that's okay. We all choose where to focus our time and energy, and not every skill needs to be mastered.

REFLECTION: PONDERING A LEARN AND SHARE JOURNEY

Some learning journeys lead to mastery, like my backhand shot. Others, like my guitar dream, remain incomplete but still shape us in meaningful ways. Whether or not we reach unconscious competence, each step of learning deepens our understanding of ourselves and the world around us.

As you reflect on this process, ponder..

What new skills or behaviors or challenges could I explore?

What will I practice until it becomes second nature?

What can I learn to be a better neighbor, employee, student, hockey player—or something else entirely?

What skills or knowledge have I already acquired that I can share or "gift" to others, just as Dave Keon inspired me all those years ago?

Who might I inspire along the way?

Water Campsite

G reat paddle...you finished the Water Element. Now imagine yourself finishing this section of the walk and setting up camp...your kitchen, your sleeping nook, your journaling/ reading/yoga space...basically the campsite that gets on the cover of Backpacker Magazine.

Again, here is an opportunity to sit and reflect on a conversation around the kitchen circle. Just an extra wee bonus pulled out of the pack...perhaps a dark chocolate bar, perhaps a small bottle of Scotch. A chance to sit back, look into a star filled sky, tell stories, laugh, confess and share life.

WATER CAMPSITE MOMENT: LETTING GO OF THE BLANKET

I had a favorite Nalgene bottle, covered in stickers that told my story—my experiences, beliefs, and perspectives. It felt like an extension of me, almost capturing the essence of who I was. And as a bonus, it glowed in the dark, making it easy to find during late-night conversations under starry skies, where there were no headlamps, lanterns, or fires—just voices sharing the quiet.

Once, while doing my final down-packing at the trailhead before a six-day hike, I realized I had left my cherished Nalgene behind in the shuttle van. I had other bottles with me, but not *that* one. The one that made me feel experienced, prepared, and uniquely me. After all, didn't the stickers prove my trail savvy and hard-earned wisdom?

And of course, that glow-in-the-dark feature—it always impressed the novices.

For a moment, I felt an unexpected sense of loss. How could I hike—let alone guide—without the comfort and confidence it brought me? The feelings reminded me of childhood comforts—a beloved blanket, a stuffed animal, or a bedtime routine that made the world feel safe.

Later, as we began our hike in the dark, I shared these feelings with my trailmates. I asked them to recall the "comforts" that got them through the days and nights of childhood and its challenges. Then, I encouraged them to reflect on the things, beliefs, and practices that help them cope with life as adults. Finally, I posed these questions:

What do you need to let go of—on the trail or back home?

What should you release to walk lighter and freer?

Now, I ask you to reflect on the same:

What possession, practice, or perspective do I cling to in an unhealthy way to help me cope?

How can I loosen my grip or let go?

WATER CAMPSITE...REFLECTIONS, WONDERINGS, PONDERINGS, DOODLINGS

Feet feeling the waves, eyes tracing the horizon. As I explore the depths, tides, and currents of being human—mentally aware and thoughtfully present—what stirs within?

What makes my heart come **ALIVE?**

What makes my soul **SING?**

What moves my spirit to **DANCE?**

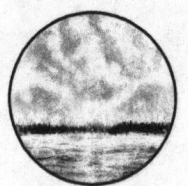

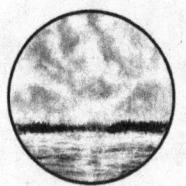

AIR

"Keep your head above water but don't forget to breathe."

ALEXI MURDOCH

Find the song, "Breathe," by Alexi Murdoch. Listen to it a few times. Let the words, the music, and their spirit percolate in your heart and mind and settle into your breath. Walk with it. Sit with it. Practice some Lectio Divina with it.

TRAIL 18

Whispers, Howls and Holding My Breath

"Awake now, he told the wind to pipe down and said to the sea, 'Quiet! Settle down!' The wind ran out of breath; the sea became smooth as glass."

"You know well enough how the wind blows this way and that. You hear it rustling through the trees, but you have no idea where it comes from or where it's headed next. That's the way it is with everyone 'born from above' by the wind of God, the Spirit of God."

JOHN 3:8

I love standing on a pier, breakwater, or beach when the wind is blowing hard—the taste, smell, and touch of salt spray from the ocean alive in the air. There's something visceral and exhilarating about it. **ALIVE!!!!** Notice *where* I love standing.

Being out on the water during a major storm? That's a different story. I've experienced it a few times. It's thrilling to have done it—but anything but fun in the moment.

Mark 4 tells a story about Jesus and his friends caught in a storm while out on the water. Give it a read. A reminder: Approach it with curiosity and imagination. Don't analyze—experience. And have fun. Wonder with me:

- What are the guys on the boat with Jesus feeling?
- How wet are they?
- How scared are they?
  What are the sounds—waves crashing, the boat creaking, sails slapping, wind howling, men shouting?
- How loud are they shouting just to be heard?
- What are they trying to communicate?
- Will the boat swamp or break apart as it heaves on a swell and pounds down into the water?
- Will the wind and waves grind it to pieces?
- How is Jesus sleeping through this?
- At what point do they realize he's asleep—and decide to wake him?
- Do they wake him thinking he can actually calm the storm, or just to help bail or steer?
- Did his command actually stop the wind and calm the water, or was it a coincidence that he spoke just as the storm ceased?
  What were the sights and sounds like when the wind stopped and the water stilled?
- How loud is the silence?
- What do their faces look like—drenched, terrified, awestruck, relieved, embarrassed?
- What did they think every time Jesus later talked about the wind or the breath of God? Did they exchange winks and glances, thinking, *"We get this, even if we don't totally get this"*?

THE ESSENCE OF LIFE

Lots of things help keep us alive and then help us live more fully—food, water, shelter, warmth, community, medicine, and more. But of all the things we need to survive, air is the most essential. Breathing is synonymous with life.

Air is the thing we can survive without for the shortest amount of time. We can face harsh conditions, endure hunger, withstand injury, and push through extreme challenges, but if we can't breathe, life slips away in minutes.

If you're like most people, you might be able to hold your breath for close to a minute, maybe a little longer. A Navy SEAL might manage two or three minutes. Harry Houdini, the famous escapologist, could hold his breath for over three minutes. The current world record stands at an astonishing 24 minutes and 37 seconds—but only after hyperventilating pure oxygen beforehand. Without that preparation, the record drops to 11 minutes and 34 seconds.

Yet even these feats show how fragile we are without air. Hold your breath too long, and your body takes over. You lose consciousness, forced to breathe by the primal drive to survive. Deprive the brain of oxygen for 3-6 minutes, and permanent damage begins. A few minutes more, and life itself ceases.

Air sustains us in ways we often take for granted. Yet its significance runs deeper than physical survival. The act of breathing and the flow of air are intimately tied to what it means to be alive.

AIR AS A SYMBOL

Since ancient times, breath and air have been powerful symbols across cultures, faiths, and philosophies. They represent what sustains us not just physically but spiritually—spirit, soul, heart, guts, being. Those things we cannot see but feel deeply.

In the Bible, the Hebrew word *ruach* first appears in Genesis 1:2: *"The Spirit of God was hovering over the waters."* It appears again in

Genesis 2:7: *"[God] breathed into his nostrils the breath of life, and the man became a living being."*

Ruach is rich with meaning, encompassing wind, breath, and spirit. It's more than the physical dynamic of air moving in and out of lungs; it carries the essence of being **alive.**

The Greek word *pneuma* carries a similar meaning. In Greek mythology, it symbolizes the breath of life itself. The New Testament continues this tradition, using *pneuma* to describe both physical breath and the Spirit of God.

When Jesus uses wind as a narrative image while speaking with Nicodemus in John 3, I wonder what he's inviting Nicodemus to ponder about the mysteries of understanding and experiencing God.

- Can't see the wind.
- Can't tell it when to blow.
- Can feel it.
- Can see the effects of its presence during and after.

Mysterious. Unpredictable. Invisible. Soothing. Scary. Inspiring. Destructive. Blows when, where, and how it wishes. Shifts, shapes, supplies.

REFLECTING ON AIR AND WIND

What is my relationship with air—with the wind?

What images, concepts, or emotions are stirred when I feel the wind?

Why is air so critical to my existence?

How important is my relationship with faith?

How vital is the dynamic of spiritual wellness in my life?

A BREATH OF INSPIRATION

"My soul is awakened, my spirit is soaring; And carried aloft on the wings of the breeze; For above and around me the wild wind is roaring."

ANNE BRONTË

"To most human beings, wind is an irritation."

MOKOKOMA MOKHONOANA

*"Wind is the most skilled hairdresser! Find a windy weather
and let your hair be shaped creatively."*

MEHMET MURAT ILDAN

*"I saw a tree dancing in the wind, and it said to me, 'I'm not
doing this to entertain you, but to remind you of what life is—a
dance in the wind!'"*

MICHAEL BASSEY JOHNSON

*"If they want me to believe in their God, they'll have to sing me
better songs...I could only believe in a God who dances."*

FRIEDRICH NIETZSCHE

PAUSE, BREATHE DEEP, AND PONDER A WORD

PSITHURISM... SITH-ERR-IZ-UM.

Let the pronunciation roll around in your vocal cords and
airways. *Sith-err-iz-um.* A word that describes the sound of wind
blowing through the trees, the rustling of leaves. I think it has a
bit of the feel and sound of what it describes. It's a good word that
evokes an even greater sound—one that stirs something deep within.

LECTIO DIVINA PRACTICE

"The leaves believe such letting go is love..."
LUCILLE CLIFTON

Find Lucille Clifton's poem, "The Lesson of the Falling Leaves." Read it a few times over. Let the words and their spirit percolate in your heart and mind and settle into your breath. Walk with it. Sit with it. Practice some Lectio Divina with it.

TRAIL 19

Spiritual
Wellness

*"Spiritual wellness is being connected to something greater
than yourself and having a set of values, principles, morals,
and beliefs that provide a sense of purpose and meaning to life,
then using those principles to guide your actions."*

EMILY SMITH

Pursuing wellness in life involves the dimensions of **mind,
body, and spirit.** It's easy to say that spiritual wellness
explores the **dimension of spirit,** but what does that truly
mean?

I think it means exploring how the inner and outer worlds
connect—helping you live into and live out a life of meaning and
purpose.

Spiritual wellness is the most intimate and personal of the
wellness dynamics. It involves nurturing the inner core of your being:
your beliefs, values, attitudes, and actions. It's about **recognizing
who you are being and who you are becoming.** It's about creating
space and pace to explore the grit and glory of life with peace and
vitality, while understanding that life is about more than just your
happiness.

Spiritual wellness doesn't mean being religious or adhering to a specific belief system. It's more than participating in religious activities, unrolling a yoga mat, or meditating. It's more than intentionally encountering nature. It is more than responsibly thinking through a swirl of behaviors, beliefs, morals and ethics. It's more than engaging in a season of letting go of and reimagining practices and perspectives of faith. It's not about subscribing to a "one-size-fits-all" approach to soul care.

It is about giving yourself **grace and permission** to explore the ordinary, extraordinary, mundane, and magnificent paths of life with a sense of reflection and action. It's recognizing life as a journey for moral reflection, intention, and compassion.

EXPLORING YOUR SPIRITUAL CORE

Here are a few hints and questions to help you explore your spiritual core:

BE CURIOUS.

What makes me feel alive?

What gives me purpose?

What helps me move through the reality of my days—especially those that are difficult and lean toward despair?

What brings me comfort?

What challenges me?

Where do faith, hope, and love fit in my days?

Exploring these thoughts often percolate mysteries, questions, doubts, or even discomfort. Don't be afraid of them, but as the saying goes, "Be curious, bot judgemental."

BE OPEN.

How do I engage with people whose beliefs and lifestyles differ from mine?

What do I do to help me understand perspectives and practices of other cultures, ethnicities, lifestyles and religions?

Seek understanding—not to condone or condemn—but to foster compassion and communication.

BE ACTIVE.

What practices and places bring me calm, strength, or encouragement?

What helps me unwind during challenging times and opens my spirit to life?

Find time, places, activities that help diminish the emotional, mental, physical stress and strain of living. Reading, biking, swimming, yoga, or simply sitting still and noticing the world. Don't make it complicated, keep it simple and nourishing

WHY SPIRITUAL WELLNESS??? A TALE OF TWO ANIMALS

Why pay attention to exploring and caring for the "spirit," this unseen part of life? Why???

- Why find intentional time to recognize and reflect on the stuff of life and the meaning of it all?
- Why nurture a purpose for life that recognizes living with compassion and care for the welfare of others and the creation?
- Why establish habits of seeking spaces of silence and solitude?
- Why encourage an understanding of good and evil, right and wrong that guides actions and attitudes?
- Why foster opportunities to reflect upon and engage in vibrant dialogue about what, why and hows of beliefs, especially with those who live with beliefs and perspectives that differ from mine?

Victor Frankl, in *Man's Search for Meaning,* wrote: *"Those who have a why to live can bear almost any how."*

The ancient book of Ecclesiastes offers a similar reminder: *"Even if you live a long time, don't take a single day for granted. Take delight in each light-filled hour, remembering there will also be many dark days, and that most of what comes your way is smoke."*

Since life is indeed a mix of **grit, grime and glory,** then perhaps the best means of navigating that mix is through having a healthy spirit that replenishes the well of "I am alive to be...."

In many Indigenous cultures, there's a story of two animals fighting within each person.

One animal embodies **joy, peace, love, hope, humility, kindness, compassion, generosity, empathy, and patience.**

The other embodies **anger, greed, regret, jealousy, arrogance, guilt, shame, pride, resentment, and negativity.**

A child asks a grandparent which animal will win.

"The one you feed," the elder replies.

When we neglect the wellness of the spirit, the grit and grime of life can breed anxiety, fear, resentment, discouragement, emptiness, apathy, self-condemnation, anger, selfishness, loss of purpose, and despair.

But when we nurture the spirit, what seems to emerge and flourish is **kindness, faithfulness, patience, hope, selflessness, optimism, self-respect, forgiveness, grace, joy, love, and a sense of mission.** Even in the midst of hard days, dark nights, and the difficulties that come with them.

A SPIRITUAL WELLNESS TEMPLATE

As mentioned earlier in the Mental Wellness trail, in the New Testament, writer Luke shares a narrative of how Jesus grew in wisdom, stature and favor with man— covering mental, physical, emotional, and social wellness dynamics. But Luke also acknowledges that Jesus grew in favor with God (Luke 2:52)—a nod to spiritual wellness.

A wandering and wondering read through some of the narratives about Jesus reveals a significant connection to spiritual wellness:

- **Birth:** A unique narrative filled with wonder, outstanding shower gifts, and a special star,
- Temple encounter at 12: Smart kid with a listening posture (Luke 2:41-52),
- **Baptism:** 18 years later,with heavens parting, doves descending, voices proclaiming. I'm imagining there is some wind at play here, symbolically and in reality (Luke 3:21–22),
- **Time in the wilderness:** Wrestling, seeking, and listening—wilderness time a valuable template for life and faith formation (Luke 4:1–13),
- **Temple proclamation:** Declaring a life mission through a reframed, redeemed, revolutionary way of viewing love and relationship with Abba and creation (Luke 4:16-21),
- **Teachings and more:** John 3:8 and John 20:22 reference wind and breath throughout a fairly significant collection

of teachings, encounters, experiences, and some miracles as well .

GUIDED BY THE SOUL

Ancient Romans and Greeks believed all people had an inner spirit, a divine presence referred to as "genius," watching over and guiding them through the entirety of life. Augustine wrote of the genius being the soul of each person and of the soul as the spiritual guide for our being, understanding, and loving.

I like to think of the soul as guiding us toward **character, calling, and mission** and ultimately compelling us to

Put love where love is not.

Kick at the darkness until the light creeps through.

Exploring and nurturing this guidance is the essence of spiritual wellness. It connects us to:

- Faith and life.
- Compassion for self and others.
- A sense of purpose and meaning.

This is where beliefs, morals, and principles merge with everyday choices and actions.

I wonder...

Where are the places I see, hear, and feel the sacred?

Where do I seek the wellness of my soul?

When do I pay attention to the wellness of my soul?

How do I care for the wellness of my soul

TRAIL 20

Whispers in the Dacks...Nurturing Sacred Space and Pace

"It is a frightful satire and an epigram on the modern age that the only use it knows for solitude is to make it a punishment, a jail sentence."

SØREN KIERKEGAARD

"For what you see and hear depends a good deal on where you are standing. It also depends on what sort of person you are."

C.S. LEWIS, THE MAGICIAN'S NEPHEW

WHISPERS IN THE DACKS
(JOURNAL ENTRY: OCTOBER 17, 2003 HIGH PEAKS WILDERNESS, ADIRONDACK PARK)

Climbing through the woods en route to the top of Mt. Marcy, the first snow of the year fell softly through the pines and firs. It felt like a scene from a grand novel or epic movie.

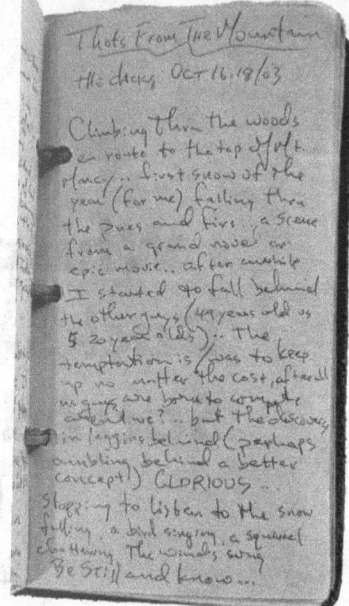

After a while, I started falling behind my trailmates. Perhaps it was the reality of being 49 and hiking with five 20-year-olds. The temptation to keep up gnawed at me. Aren't we born to compete, after all?

But then came the discovery in lagging behind—or rather, in ambling behind.

Glorious.

Stopping to listen to the snow falling. Hearing a bird sing. Noticing a squirrel chatter. The wind humming through the trees.

Be still and know.

Swallowing pride and reputation, I was blessed by the redemptive silence of the woods. My soul, heart, and mind were nurtured by El Roi's grace-filled whispering.

How often are whispers like these reaching out to us, only to go unnoticed amid the noise of our healthy and unhealthy pursuits? A position attained. A power sought. A possession yearned for. Right and wrong motives alike can drown out whispers of grace, hope, and encouragement—all sacrificed for applause, accolades, and approval.

Yet the whispers are always there. We don't need to seek them; they seek us. The snow falls. The wind sings. Whether I stop to listen and let the whispers embrace my soul is entirely my choice.

THE POWER OF STILLNESS

(Reflections from I Kings 19)

For many of us, life can be overfilled with noise litter—the sounds that crowd our spaces and squeeze our souls. Research shows this noise increases anxiety, blood pressure, heart disease, and a general unwellness and malaise.

I invite you to pause. To consider the acoustic detritus cluttering your path. To create and curate a space and pace to hear the whispers of nature's voice. To embrace the posture of, *"Be still and know..."*

I appreciate the narrative of Elijah in I Kings 19:1-13. His life is swirling with fear, confusion, anger, and anxiety. He's angry at Yahweh and people, overwhelmed and desperate for clarity.

I appreciate the posture of him going out to stand on the mountain, believing that Yahweh was about to pass by.

I appreciate the position of him needing to hear a gracious, calming voice in the midst of his turmoil.

I appreciate the imagery of that voice coming—but not in the powerful wind that ripped mountains apart and shattered rocks, nor the earthquake or fire that followed.

No. It is in the *still, small voice—the gentle whisper*—that Yahweh speaks.

As Donald Miller writes in *Blue Like Jazz*: "Too much of our time is spent trying to chart God on a grid and too little time is spent allowing our hearts to feel awe... We want to predict, dissect, and manage God. But wonder comes when we let go of answers and maps, making space for awe."

CURATING THE WHISPERS

In Exodus 3:1-14, Moses, a shepherd, notices a bush on fire but not consumed. When he slows down enough to truly look, he stops. In that pause, he experiences a space saturated with awe, wonder, meaning, grace, hope, and significance.

I remember a personal moment of stopping in the desert wilderness, minus the burning bush.

After a long, hot day of hiking desert trails, I found a place to camp near a slow-moving river. Exhausted, I laid my head down to stare at the stars. Just as I was drifting to sleep, a small breeze brushed my face.

My overwhelming thought at that moment was that my cheek had been kissed by El Roi—the God who sees me.

It may not have been as dramatic as a burning bush, but it was a moment. A kiss. Saturated with grace, hope, and meaning.

These moments, whether ancient or personal, invite us to slow down and pay attention to the sacred. They call us to nurture a posture of awe and wonder.

PRACTICES TO NURTURE AWE AND WONDER

Let me suggest and invite you to consider the same practices I experienced that snowy morning in the deep woods of the Adirondacks—practices that can nurture the space and pace of awe and wonder.

1. Silence

When, where, and how do I quiet my life?

Noise surrounds us, cluttering minds and spirits. A space and pace of silence can be a path to listening. In moments of quiet, we can hear the whispers filled with awe, meaning, and grace.

2. Solitude

When, where, and how do I embrace solitude to seed calmness, peace, and understanding?

Step away from the noise and demands of life and into a space of solitude. Solitude invites reflection and connection with self and sacred.

3. Slowing

When, where, and how do I slow life down to listen and see—for the wellness of myself and others?

Slowing requires intentionality in a world of fast. Whether it's lagging behind on a hike to listen to the snowfall or camping by a river under the stars, slowing allows us to notice grace. It makes room for the divine brush of presence, the gentle whisper that refreshes our weary spirits.

4. Stopping and Soaking Up

What do I do with what I see, hear, and feel in these spaces?

Stopping is an act of trust and surrender. It's the choice to pause, even when life beckons us forward. Stopping creates sacred moments—spaces to see, hear, and feel what we might otherwise miss. And soaking up invites us to fully embrace these moments, letting awe, grace, and purpose transform and guide how we live in the world.

Take time to practice silence, solitude, slowing, stopping, and soaking up. Amid the noise of life, nurture the space and pace to hear the whispers of grace calling out to you.

AND SPEAKING OF WHISPERS...
WHISPERS OF TRUTH

"The gunfire around us makes it hard to hear. But the human voice is different from other sounds. It can be heard over noises that bury everything else. Even when it's not shouting. Even

when it's just a whisper. Even the lowest whisper can be heard over armies... when it's telling the truth."

EDMUND ZUWANIE IN THE INTERPRETER (2005)

How do I discern the truth?

What distracts me from the whispers?

What truth am I using my voice for?

"To stand for the truth, for that silent thing that most kindly haunts us, feels like leaving the party for a time out, going into a cold, dark room alone. How many times have we chosen the lights over the loneliness"

STEVE GARNAAS-HOLMES

LECTIO DIVINA PRACTICE

"Courage is with me
When I seek for the truth
When I speak for the truth
When I stand for the truth."

ROSE MARIE JUAN-AUSTIN

Find Rose Marie Juan-austin's poem Courage and Truth. Read it a few times. Let the words and spirit of it percolate in your heart and mind. Walk with it. Sit with it. Practice some Lectio Divina with it.

A Tribute to a Still Man

The practices of silence, solitude, slowing, and stopping to soak up life are not just transformative for our own souls. They also shape how we move through the world, impacting the lives of those we encounter. In cultivating these postures, we create a sacred space for others—a space where they can experience calm, grace, and the freedom to grow into who they are meant to be.

I was blessed to experience such a space through the life of a mentor, a man whose stillness and grace left an indelible mark on me. His life served as a testament to how sacred stillness can ripple outward, influencing not just one person but entire communities.

One of the blessings we can bring into people's lives is the space to be still, to be honest, and to simply be.

This comes when we recognize each person's uniqueness—their abilities, gifts, and yes, their quirks. (And believe me, we all have our quirks. Some might say I ended up with more than my fair share!) But creating that space requires resisting the compulsion to force or form a person into what we think they should be.

At times I have bumped up against systems that said there was a "right way" to act, speak, lead, dress, and even choose a method of transportation. Apparently, in some circles, bikes and trucks were not considered pastoral or professional enough. Failure to conform is often labeled rebellious or detrimental.

Too often, people are dismissed or diminished simply because they don't fit someone else's expectations. And that's a loss for everyone.

I work, play, and live as a pilgrimage guide. My role is to create spaces where people can encounter both the sacred and the mundane—spaces where the grit and glory of raw humanity meet the beauty of a holy relationship with Creator and creation. Allowing people to walk as they were created to be, rather than as I think they should be, is a space I hold as truly sacred.

I experienced this space and then learned to cultivate it from my mentor, Stillman Cameron.

STILL MAN

Stillman Cameron was, in every sense, a still man. He practiced silence, solitude, slowing, and being still and knowing. He was a man of grace, strength, and courage; a man of wisdom, kindness, and compassion. He carried humor, patience, and self-control in equal measure.

Through a series of unexpected circumstances, Stillman and I ended up working together at a church in a small town in New Brunswick Canada. He was the senior pastor, and I was the youth pastor. It didn't take long to see what a remarkable gentleman he was.

Three weeks into my new role, I had an experience that would significantly shape my understanding of grace and guidance.

A CHRISTMAS CAROL IN JULY

Back in those days, it was common to have a Sunday evening service that was unique from the Sunday morning one. We just couldn't get enough church into our lives, I guess. As the youth pastor, one of my tasks was to introduce the hymns for the evening service.

This was back in the days of hymnals, and limited understanding and practice of the concept of a "worship leader".

My job was simple: announce the hymn number, trust the pianist and organist to carry the tune, and step back from the mic.

But I wasn't one to do things in a predictable, beige manner and so I decided to spice the evening up a bit. It was the last Sunday of July and I thought it would be fun to do a Christmas carol. However, I didn't want it to be without intentionality, so I spent the afternoon going through the hymnbook, pulling together a series of hymns that walked us through the story of Jesus. (Yes, "Tell Me The Story of Jesus" was one of them.) Birth, life, death, resurrection, ascension, mission...everything was covered. It was creative, intentional, and perhaps a little ambitious. Something to understand here is that I have a propensity to collect a significant amount of random things that all have a place and purpose in my life, but tend to create a wee bit of clutter. I also can too easily veer into the lane of why tell two stories when you have five good ones. Unfortunately I veered and cluttered that evening.

That July evening seemed no different at first. Service started at 7 and was generally done a few minutes after 8. However, by the time we got to the early days of Jesus's ministry, the clock was ticking and ticking fast.

MASTER CRAFTSMAN

It's important to note that Stillman Cameron was a master craftsman in the pulpit. He was a student of the scriptures, deeply in love with God's Story and with the people who sat under his teaching each week. He approached preaching with both passion and discipline, pouring equal effort into his Sunday morning and evening sermons.The temptation of many a preacher in those days was to serve the best wine (perhaps not the best metaphor for dry congregations) Sunday morning and get by with the dregs at the bottom of the barrel Sunday night. Not Stillman.

All that to say, he was PREPARED that Sunday night and it was going to be GOOD.

Unfortunately, by the time I got past the resurrection and ascension and brought the music portion of the service to an end, it was 7:57. Three weeks into this new position, and I had blown it. Even though it may have been an inspiring and educational walk through the life of Jesus, it was way off script, and I hadn't prepared Stillman or myself for such an extended time. I had blown it and left him in a difficult situation.

I sat down (in those days we pastors sat on the platform behind the pulpit during the service) embarrassed and feeling like...well you can guess how I felt. What had I done? What was I thinking? His third Sunday with this new congregation, with a sermon he had prayed and worked hard to prepare, and I'd thrown him behind the proverbial 8 ball.

Stillman rose from his seat, walked to the pulpit, and began:

"I have a three-point sermon on Zacchaeus tonight.

Point 1: Zacchaeus was a short man. So am I.

Point 2: Zacchaeus was up a tree. So am I.

Point 3: Zacchaeus came down. And so am I."

With that, he turned and walked off the platform. As he passed my chair, he tilted his head and with an impish smile and a wink and a nod, he said, "Come on, son."

A LESSON IN GRACE

Stillman and I walked down the center aisle and into the foyer together to meet the congregation as they left. As we did, he leaned over and whispered, "That was a great service, son. Well done."

Later that evening, I sat in Stillman and Ethel's basement, my clumsy attempts at apologizing for leaving him in such a predicament rebuffed by both each time I attempted.

"Nothing to apologize for," Stillman said. "It was a wonderful service. We make a great team. Did you see the looks on their faces when we walked down the aisle? Delightful."

That night, Stillman taught me lessons that have stayed with me since: be flexible, be gracious, and don't underestimate the power of encouragement. And maybe pick four songs instead of twelve. Most importantly, he showed me the value of creating space for someone to grow into themselves—quirks, missteps, and all.

He nurtured a space where a bumbling, quirky, creative, eager young man was encouraged to be himself, to live into the gifts and abilities and strengths and even weaknesses that he had. Thank you, Stillman Cameron, for believing in me rather than stifling me. Thank you for your grace and guidance. I've tried to pay it forward every chance I've had.

PONDER

Who are the Still Men and Women in my life? The mentors, guides, and companions who have nurtured a space and pace for me to grow, quirks and all?

How might I cultivate a similar gift for others—whether through stillness, grace, or simply showing up with compassion and humor?

A Spiritual Wellness Ponder

"Behold God beholding you... and smiling."

ANTHONY DE MELLO

One of the hardest days for some people on the pilgrimages I guide is the day I ask them to imagine walking in the presence of a loving El Roi—the God who sees them—a perfect expression of both mother and father.

The challenge lies in the invitation: to walk through the woods, city streets, or desert pathways while soaking up what El Roi says s/he likes about them.

Why is this so difficult? Because it's far easier for many to hear the voice of condemnation. We usually default to assume God sees what is awful, shameful, or broken about them. Guilt, shame, and disgust often dominate the inner dialogue about how we think God views them.

A NEW PERSPECTIVE

But what if I walk with a different belief?
"Behold God beholding me... and smiling!"
The dynamic shifts when I allow myself to imagine a grace-filled presence—a God who delights in me. It's not always easy to embrace this. Letting grace take hold of my heart and mind can feel like a struggle. Yet, when I do, the change is profound.

So let me suggest this practice: Find a space and pace that feel right for you. Walk with El Roi and listen. Truly listen. Let yourself hear the sacred whispers of a loving Abba.

A LOVING INVITATION

As you walk, reflect on these questions:
What does El Roi like about me?

What gifts has Abba given me to embrace and share with a needy world?

What strengths do I carry that deserve to be acknowledged and nurtured?

Now imagine Abba saying:
"Yes, you are wired uniquely, but I am the One who wired you. I didn't get it wrong."

PAUSE AND REFLECT

How does that make me feel?

What does it make me think?

And how does it change the way I respond to a world that desperately needs love—love placed where love is not?

THE INVITATION TO WALK

This practice of walking with El Roi is an invitation to see yourself as you truly are—through the eyes of divine love. Let it fill you, transform you, and flow out into the world.

Take time to listen.

Take time to walk.

And let grace embrace you.

Star Gazing and Faith Wrestling

"Ah, the universal Jesus—no Jew, no Greek, no in, no out. Just an invitation to wrestle with grace. To have your hip wrenched by it. Compelled to lay back and gaze at the stars, wondering if this might be a good time to build an altar."

JEFF TROTTER, CANYON TRAILMATE

In the American Southwest, there's a wild canyon I've wandered nearly 40 times in a pilgrimage posture. Over about 200 days and nights, I've walked close to 2,000 miles of desert trails, curated intentionally to explore my relationship with faith, life, and El Roi—the God who sees me.

Many of those steps have been taken with a limp—sometimes physical, but more often soul-deep. I carry with me the story of Jacob wrestling with God:

"Because you have struggled with God and humans and have overcome... I saw God face to face, and lived to tell the story."
—Genesis 32:28, 30

My Osprey Kestrel backpack holds the physical essentials: food, water, shelter, clothing. My soul, however, carries its own load—a pack brimming with questions, ponderings, struggles, pains, fears, doubts, vulnerabilities, curses, and tears. Yet alongside these, my soul carries discoveries, delights, laughter, gratitude, and celebration—a collision and collection of humanity and grace.

Wrestling with Grace a deep awareness of the darkness encroaching

I walk with loneliness, hunger, exhaustion, and that deep awareness—but also with companionship, sustenance, and the surprising lightness that comes with grace. It's a messy, beautiful swirl of grit and glory, grime and grace, all ground together by life's rhythm.

Frederick Buechner described Jacob's encounter by the river as the *"magnificent defeat of the human soul at the hands of God."* A defeat that blesses—a discovery of presence, of faith, of something deeper.

The times of star-gazing and faith-wrestling matter deeply for the wellness of my spirit. They nurture my soul, offering space and pace to lean into mystery, to sit with questions, seekings, and doubts, all while leaving room for grace-filled, unexpected discoveries.

A DESERT PILGRIMAGE

The canyon trail I walk follows a small, winding river. Along its sandy banks, I often see signs of mule deer, bighorn sheep, and mountain cats coming to drink. Their presence always calls to mind the psalm:

"As the deer desires rivers of water, so my soul desires You, O God."
—Psalm 42:1

The hours and miles spent walking under the desert sun create a thirst far different from anything I experience at home. This is a deeper, sometimes desperate thirst that propels me toward the springs scattered along the way. Here, **desire becomes a compelling force,** not just for water but for encounters that quench something soul-deep. Thirst and longing shape the questions I carry.

And at night lying in the sand by the river under the canopy of desert stars, I wrestle and wonder and desire.

A PRACTICE...

As I thirst and desire, I engage with my faith through... **WRESTLING. SEARCHING. PROBING. ENGAGING. DOUBTING. QUESTIONING. LAUGHING. CRYING. STROLLING. SITTING. LISTENING**

And I craft and curate times to seek...
Is there hunger and thirst in my life for something deeper?

What is my faith asking of me?

What fight is worth wrestling for in my faith?

What doubt needs exploring?

What discovery is waiting to be embraced?

When do I sense that life is sacred and worthwhile?

What song is my faith singing?

What is truly worth living for—not just for a time, but for a lifetime?

Can I trust **El Roi** with the unknown—and let the mysteries remain mysteries?

AN INVITATION

This practice is not about answers but about making space to wrestle with the questions. It is not necessary to hike through a canyon or find a remote plateau to lay back and star gaze to embrace this practice. It's about finding moments to metaphorically gaze at the stars and to sit by the river. And it's about finding actual space and pace in your life to wonder at the sacred, and to embrace the magnificent defeat that is somehow also the greatest blessing.

Let yourself wrestle. Let yourself wonder.

And maybe, just maybe, you'll find it's a good time to build an altar.

LECTIO DIVINA PRACTICE

"In my doubt, in all my weakness...and I'll find peace beneath the shadow of your wings"

MALIBU

Find the song Malibu by Mumford and Sons. Listen to it a few times. Let the words, the music, and their spirit percolate in your heart and mind and settle into your breath. Walk with it. Sit with it. Practice some Lectio Divina with it.

Exploring Faith as a Verb

The reality of raw, naked faith often calls the pilgrim to leave behind what is nailed down, obvious, and secure—to walk into the unknown, following the invitation to "Follow me."

Faith, in its noun form, is typically defined as:

- A great trust or confidence in something or someone.
- A strong belief in God or a particular religion.

But faith is so much more than a static definition. It's a word that stirs thoughts, beliefs, practices, concepts, and conversations—a word that can inspire, challenge, or even unsettle us. Faith is not a word to fear, nor should it be confined to a rigid framework of answers.

At its heart, faith is rooted in trust and confidence, but it also invites us to take a journey, to walk an uncharted path of exploration. It often begins as a noun but is lived out in the form of a verb. It grows in the fertile ground of conversation and community, catalyzed by the act of questioning. It is much more about action than definition.

Just as a compelling story finds its pulse in anguished questions, so too does a vibrant faith journey. It requires the courage to wrestle with uncertainty and embrace the mysteries of love and grace. For Jacob, faith was a journey of bold questions and wrestling—one marked by confidence in the One with whom he wrestled.

LECTIO DIVINA PRACTICE

"Ask the questions that have no answers... Be like the fox who makes more tracks than necessary, some in the wrong direction."

WENDELL BERRY

Find Wendell Berry's poem, "Manifesto: The Mad Farmer Liberation Front." Read it slowly, more than once. Let its words and spirit percolate in your heart and mind. Walk with it. Sit with it. Practice *Lectio Divina* with it. Allow his words to speak to you, challenge you, and invite you into deeper reflection.

A STROLL AND A CONVERSATION

Now consider "Manifesto: The Mad Farmer Liberation Front." this alongside Terry Tempest Williams' powerful declaration:

"This is my living faith, an active faith, a faith of verbs: to question, explore, experiment, experience, walk, run, dance, play, eat, love, learn, dare, taste, touch, smell, listen, speak, write, read, draw, provoke, emote, scream, sin, repent, cry, kneel, pray, bow, rise, stand, look, laugh, cajole, create, confront, confound, walk back, walk forward, circle, hide, and seek."

FROM LEAP BY TERRY TEMPEST WILLIAMS

Imagine a meandering walk with Wendell Berry, Terry Tempest Williams, yourself, and a perhaps a close friend of yours. The conversation drifts to faith:

What does faith mean to each of you?

How do you personally explore and nurture faith?

How does faith guide and shape your life?

What role do mystery and questions play in a life of faith?

Now, turn the conversation inward. As you wander and wonder about the role of faith in your own life, what are the thoughts emerging from the stroll.

QUESTIONS TO CARRY

As you reflect, consider these questions:

What does it mean for faith to be active—a verb—in my life?

How is faith informing my actions, choices, and relationships?

Am I creating space in your life to wrestle with questions and mystery?

What does the interplay of doubt and trust look like in my faith journey?

Am I, and how am I nurturing a living, growing faith?

AN INVITATION TO ACTION

Faith is not meant to sit idle as a static noun—it invites us into motion, action, and exploration. Take a step today, whether physical or metaphorical, to embody faith as a verb. Question, explore, experiment, and engage with the world and the sacred.

Let yourself imagine, wrestle, and wonder.

And, as Wendell Berry suggests, don't be afraid to make a few tracks in the wrong direction along the way.

TRAIL 25

A Path to Explore

"It is a world of magic and mystery, of deep darkness and
flickering starlight. It is a world where terrible things happen
and wonderful things too. It is a world where goodness is pitted
against evil, love against hate, order against chaos, in a great
struggle where often it is hard to be sure who belongs to which
side because appearances are endlessly deceptive. Yet for all
its confusion and wildness, it is a world where the battle goes
ultimately to the good, who live happily ever after, and where
in the long run everybody, good and evil alike, becomes known
by his true name... That is the fairy tale of the Gospel with, of
course, one crucial difference from all other fairy tales, which
is that the claim made for it is that it is true, that it not only
happened once upon a time but has kept on happening ever
since and is happening still."

FREDERICK BUECHNER, TELLING THE TRUTH: THE GOSPEL AS
TRAGEDY, COMEDY, AND FAIRY TALE

A FAITH IN TENSION

Is faith the opposite of certainty and predictability? Faith, at its best, is not a rigid certainty but a journey into the unknown. **Trail 30** explored the wrestling between grace and struggle—a raw, vulnerable engagement with life and its questions under the stars. **Trail 31** invited us to live faith as a verb—an active, evolving practice rather than a static definition. What happens when the stories we once embraced bump into unsolved mysteries or even doubts?

Faith often starts as something nailed down—a fixed certainty in our lives. But as we grow, it is not uncommon for that once-clear faith to face questions, challenges, and mysteries. Now, we stand at another crossroad. What happens when the certainty of past beliefs collides with the complexity of present realities? When the stories we once embraced begin to feel fragile under the weight of mystery? Faith, once defined by answers, becomes something to be lived in the tension of questions.

A TALE OF CERTAINTY

When my granddaughters still believed in Santa Claus, Ella—the elder sister—approached Laura (mom) and David (dad), confessing she'd figured out the truth: Santa Claus was them. She assured them, however, that she would keep the ruse alive for the sake of her younger sister Rosie. "Your secret is safe with me," she said confidently.

But only weeks later, Rosie approached her parents. "I know it's you," she announced, "but I don't want to spoil it for Ella. Your secret is safe with me."

What do we do when the stories we once held tightly begin to unravel? Santa Claus. The Easter Bunny. The Tooth Fairy. The Great Pumpkin. They're often the first fables to fade, paving the way for us to question the bigger stories we've been told. For those raised in a faith tradition, the unraveling can feel disorienting. Stories of whales and giants, battles won with trumpets and clay jars, fiery furnaces, lion's dens and parted seas—what do we do when the faith tales of childhood begin to feel more like fairy tales? Were these just fables told to control us? For me, the stories were told on flannelgraph boards (look it up on Google). T'was a delightful way of storytelling. But delightful or not, what happens when the certainty they offered can no longer hold up against the complexities of adult life?

TWO PATHS OFT TAKEN

I have noticed a couple of paths that are often explored at this intersection of life.

Path 1: Certainty over curiosity. This path clings tightly to tradition and heritage, sometimes with blind loyalty. Certainty is prioritized, and the unknown feels threatening. Questions are suppressed, mysteries tapped down and left unexplored.

Path 2: Rejection over engagement. This path rejects the faith of the past entirely. Certainty becomes an enemy, and the stories, practices, community, and beliefs are discarded wholesale— sometimes with anger, frustration, and even defiance. (Sometimes with an emphatic expression involving a finger thrust to the sky. And just to clarify, not the "One way, Jesus" index finger.)

A NARROW PATH...THE PATH LESS TAKEN

I like to wander a third path—one where mysteries, questions, confusions, doubts, and pains of life are not obstacles but companions. I wander it with the posture of a curious heart, mind, and soul.

It's a path that resonates with the invitation to walk with a carpenter-rabbi 2,000 years ago—he who told stories, asked questions, and pointed toward life on a narrow, adventurous road.

This path is not about certainty but about trust. It invites us to embrace questions rather than fear them, to navigate mystery without demanding clarity. It's a way of living faith as an ongoing exploration—a place where doubts and wonderings can shape us, not break us.

Faith on this path becomes an adventure—a pursuit of grace, not answers, and an engagement with life's tensions that leads not to resolution, but to deeper life. This is not a path to quick answers or tidy resolutions. It is one of patience and process, of faith held not as certainty but as hope—faith as the act of walking forward.

FAITH TALE OR FAIRY TALE??? HMMMM????

As you consider this narrow path, reflect on these questions:
Is my faith more rooted in certainty or exploration?

How do faith and doubt interact in my life?

What mysteries and questions am I afraid to explore?

Am I clinging to answers or open to trusting the unknown?

Am I on Path 1, 2, or 3—and why?

What does a life of faith as exploration and trust look like for me?

Where is my faith evolving, and where am I resisting?

AN INVITATION

I invite you to walk the path of exploration and trust, navigating life's questions, mysteries, and dilemmas with an open heart. Let go of the need for certainty and step into the tension of faith—a journey of wandering and wondering.

LECTIO DIVINA PRACTICE

*"We are impatient of being on the way to something unknown,
something new.
And yet it is the law of all progress
that it is made by passing through some stages of instability—
and that it may take a very long time..."*

PIERRE TEILHARD DE CHARDIN

Find Pierre Teilhard de Chardin's poem, "Patient Trust." Read it a few times. Let the words and spirit of it percolate in your heart and mind. Walk with it. Sit with it. Practice some Lectio Divina with it.

Financial Wellness

PERSPECTIVES ON MONEY AND SPIRITUALITY

There are countless perspectives on what financial wellness entails. It's often defined as the ability to plan for and manage money, leading to improved quality of life and increased wealth. This includes skills like budgeting, saving, and investing to secure both present and future stability. Try saying all that five times fast with a mouthful of marshmallows!

But let me suggest a different perspective: What if we approached exploring financial wellness through the lens of spiritual wellness?

"When there is money in your hand and not in your heart, it will not harm you even if it is a lot; and when it is in your heart, it will harm you even if there is none in your hands."

IBN QAYYIM AL-JAWZIYYA

"If you mistreat the poor, you insult your Creator; if you are kind to them, you show Him respect."

PROVERBS 14:31

"Money is like love—it kills slowly and painfully the one who withholds it, and enlivens the one who turns it on his fellow man."

KAHLIL GIBRAN

"For the love of money is the root of all evil."

1 TIMOTHY 6:10

Money has been at the center of human connection and conflict for as long as stories have been told. From Disney classics like *Aladdin; Robin Hood;* and *Cinderella* to modern films like *The Wolf of Wall Street; The Big Short;* and *Lock, Stock,* and *Two Smoking Barrels,* we're reminded of the siren call of riches.

Money shapes relationships, cultures, and systems. It can serve us—or enslave us. Similarly, at the core of humanity lies our relationship with spirituality. In major religions and folk traditions alike—from the *Tanakh* (Judaism) to the *Rigveda* (Hinduism), the *Dhammapada* (Buddhism), the *Quran* (Islam), and the Bible (Christianity), money is addressed as a potential danger, a responsibility, and a tool for compassionate care.

These texts emphasize charity, kindness, simplicity, virtuous character, and social action—especially for the poor. A common thread is the invitation to cultivate a passion for life rather than for wealth, leading to compassion that stewards our resources to make the world better.

JESUS AND FINANCIAL WELLNESS

The Bible contains over 2,300 verses about money, wealth, and possessions, and more than 2,000 references to the poor.

Although there's debate about how many parables Jesus told (38, 39, 46, or perhaps a few more or less), it's widely acknowledged that eleven of them deal with money or finances. This has led some to claim that Jesus talked about money more than any other topic. Factually, this may be correct, but I suggest caution before concluding that finances were his primary focus. Perhaps Jesus used money as an illustration to get people thinking about deeper perspectives.

Take, for instance, Jesus' relationship to poverty: two pigeons offered at his purification ceremony instead of a lamb, no place to lay his head, part-time carpentry, and borrowed items (a boat, food to multiply, a donkey, and even a tomb). At the same time, he seemed at ease with wealth: accepting costly gifts, attending elaborate feasts, and gaining the reputation of eating and drinking to the point of being called a glutton and drunkard.

His parables often invite layered interpretations. Consider the parable of the talents (Matthew 25). In many traditions, this parable is understood as a lesson on stewardship (especially for church building campaigns), with the heroes being the servants who doubled their money. Yet, in some cultures, it's interpreted as a critique of oppressive systems or empires. In this view, the master is harsh and absent, building his empire on the back of others, embodying the antithesis of Jesus' teachings about Abba. Here, the Christ figure is the servant who refused to participate in the system and paid with his life.

So, which interpretation is correct? Perhaps both?

FINANCIAL WELLNESS AS A LOVE-MY-NEIGHBOR EXPLORATION

This "perhaps both?" complexity reflects the nuanced conversations required when exploring finances from a spiritual perspective. Much depends on upbringing, life experiences, cultural context, and religious beliefs. What is clear across cultures and traditions, however, is the emphasis on how we treat the poor and the invitation to live with compassion rather than consumption.

If we explore financial wellness through a spiritual lens, it becomes less about personal wealth-building and more about communal well-being. It's a "love my neighbor" exploration, where our financial practices align with values of kindness, charity, and justice.

John Wesley, in his 18th-century sermon *"The Use of Money,"* offered three guiding principles:

Earn all you can.

Save all you can.

Give all you can.

"Get all you can without hurting your soul, your body, or your neighbor. Save all you can, cutting off every needless expense. Give all you can. Be glad to give, and ready to distribute; laying up in store for yourselves a good foundation against the time to come, that you may attain eternal life."

Wesley's emphasis was always on the third. Yes, make all you can but not at the expense of others or your own being. Yes, save all you can, but not by stashing it away for a rainy day. Rather, by buying and living wisely rather than wastefully. But ultimately, it all came down to being generous and giving.

He claimed, "Money is an excellent gift of God, answering the noblest ends. In the hands of His children, it is food for the hungry, drink for the thirsty, raiment for the naked."

PAUSE AND CONTEMPLATE FINANCIAL WELLNESS AND THE SPIRITUAL JOURNEY

This trail invites you to explore financial wellness as more than balance sheets and savings accounts. It's a path of discovering how money, when guided by grace and compassion, can serve as a tool for love, justice, and communal flourishing.

Stewardship. Stability. Strength. Risk management. Short-term profits. Sustainability. Responsibility. Bottom line. Serving society. Arrogance. Fear. Greed. Retirement. Credit. Debt. Budget. Financial goals.

What thoughts, questions, or emotions do these words stir in my mind and heart?

What are my attitudes about finances?

What are my practices with finances?

How do I react to the uses and abuses of money?

If I had the power to reset the world's financial system, what would I change—and why?

LECTIO DIVINA PRACTICE

"Sit down wherever you are
And listen to the wind singing in your veins.
Feel the love, the longing, the fear in your bones."

JOHN WELWOOD

Find John Welwood's poem, "Forget About Entitlement." Read it a few times. Let the words and spirit of it percolate in your heart and mind. Walk with it. Sit with it. Practice some Lectio Divina with it.

Air Campsite

B reathe deep...you finished the Air Element. Now imagine yourself finishing this section of the walk and setting up camp...your kitchen, your sleeping nook, your journaling/reading/yoga space...basically the campsite that gets on the cover of Backpacker Magazine.

We've reached your next opportunity to sit and reflect on a conversation around the kitchen circle. Just an extra wee bonus pulled out of the pack...perhaps a dark chocolate bar, perhaps a small bottle of Scotch. A chance to sit back, look into a star filled sky, tell stories, laugh, confess and share life.

AIR CAMPSITE MOMENT: PACKING LIFE'S BACKPACK

After the third or fourth day on a backpacking pilgrimage, I often ask these questions around a campfire or supper circle..
What did I bring that I wish I had left behind?

What do I wish I had brought?

What are some things I have that are invaluable treasures for this experience?

This leads to a broader exercise:

Pack your metaphorical backpack for life's journey.

What are your 5 essential, non-negotiable must-haves?

What are 5 non-essentials you've carried too long and are ready to leave behind?

   Try this exercise as a self-reflection and perhaps as a contemplative conversation with a few "life trailmates." During the "trailmates" conversation, strive for consensus on your lists.

   Here are a few suggested "backpacks" to consider:

Faith
Family
Community
Life
Vocation

Bonus conversation: What is one thing in today's world that you would take out of the "world's backpack," and why?

ESSENTIALS   NON-ESSENTIALS

AIR CAMPSITE MOMENT: AWE AND WON-DER

"There are two ways to live: you can live as if nothing is a miracle; you can live as if everything is a miracle. The most beautiful thing we can experience is the mysterious. It is the source of all true art and all science. He to whom this emotion is a stranger, who can no longer pause to wonder and stand rapt in awe, is as good as dead: his eyes are closed."

ALBERT EINSTEIN

"Wisdom begins in wonder."

SOCRATES

"Awe is the feeling of being in the presence of something vast that transcends your current understanding of the world... Wonder, the mental state of openness, questioning, curiosity, and embracing mystery, arises out of experiences of awe... people who find more everyday awe show evidence of living with wonder. They are more open to new ideas. To what language can't describe."

DACHER KELTNER, AWE: THE NEW SCIENCE OF EVERYDAY WONDER

"Our goal should be to live life in radical amazement... get up in the morning and look at the world in a way that takes nothing for granted. Everything is phenomenal; everything is incredible; never treat life casually. To be spiritual is to be amazed."

ABRAHAM JOSHUA HESCHEL

Aweandwonder...stepintostopsoakupwithinha leexhaleand againbreathinglifegivinginspiredmo mentsdrenchedandsaturatedwithmeaninggrace hopesignificance...ALIVE!!!

When...

Where...

Why...

How...

What...

Who...

AIR CAMPSITE - REFLECTIONS, WONDE-RINGS, PONDERINGS, DOODLINGS

Feet following the paths of the wind, ears attuned to the breath of the trees. As I explore the whispers, depths, and soul of being human—spiritually aware and fully present—what do I discover?

What makes my heart come ALIVE?

What makes my soul SING?

What moves my spirit to DANCE?

FIRE

LECTIO DIVINA PRACTICE

"What makes a fire burn is space between the logs, a breathing space..."

JUDY BROWN

Find Judy Brown's poem, "Fire." Read it a few times. Let the words and spirit of it percolate in your heart and mind. Walk with it. Sit with it. Practice some Lectio Divina with it.

Stories, S'mores, and Symbols

"Of the four elements—earth, fire, water, and air—fire is the ardent brother. Despite its tumultuous temperament, despite the fact that it is composed not only of benevolent but also malicious powers, of these four elemental 'siblings,' it is fire that mankind has always been able to identify with best. Like us, fire is one of the living—a living, upright creature. It is born, needs nourishment and oxygen, it ages, and dies."

JULIE DAMGAARD PIO DIAZ

Fire...what images come to your mind? What memories? What thoughts? What words or phrases?

- Stories and songs shared around a campfire.
- Comforting warmth.
- S'mores and marshmallows roasting over open flames.
- Mesmerizing gazes.
- Flames of a candle, a crackling fireplace, or a wood stove.

Fire brings life, yet it also destroys. It invites silent reflection and creates magical moments. It is beautiful and terrifying—consuming, formative, creative, and cleansing.

I wonder what it was like to discover fire for the very first time. To feel its warmth.

To witness its power to consume and transform.

To explore its essential presence for living through days and nights.

I wonder about the fears, emotions, practical uses, and sacred imaginings that this discovery evoked.

From that first discovery, fire has been a vital presence in human history. It has lit paths, warmed homes, and cooked meals. But it has also served as an compelling image:

- A burning bush.
- A pillar of fire guiding the way.
- The Olympic torch.
- Jehovah on Mount Sinai.
- Funeral pyres and purification rituals.

Across traditions—whether Indigenous beliefs, Greek mythology, sacred texts, or countless other articulations of human history—fire has been a significant symbol and expression of passion, transformation, creation, and destruction. It often points to something sacred, something holy.

Fire reminds me to pause and be present—to see its flames as a reflection of the divine presence.

Though I haven't seen or heard Yahweh in the realm of physical reality—no burning bushes, no pillars or tongues of fire, no audible James Earl Jones-type voice—I've had moments where I've sensed the sacred and felt as though I were in the presence of Yahweh.

I wonder about the places, moments, and tangible experiences that draw me into that sense of sacred presence—a connection to the divine.

What about you?

Fire.

Light. Warmth. Guidance. Cooking. Refining. Transformation. Consuming. Dangerous. Fear. Judgment. Respect.

When I think about fire and the sacred, what stirs in my mind and heart?

Let the campfire invite you into this sacred practice of presence. Watch the flames flicker and dance. Listen to the crackle. Notice how it burns but also draws us together—warming hearts and illuminating paths.

SIT BY THE FIRE AND PONDER

Let these words spark imagination, ignite spirit, and invite reflection on the fire within and around.

The most powerful weapon on earth is the human soul on fire.
FERDINAND FOCH

Set your life on fire. Seek those who fan your flames.
RUMI

In everyone's life, at some time, our inner flame goes out. It is then burst into flame by an encounter with another human being. We should all be thankful for those people who rekindle the inner spirit.

ALBERT SCHWEITZER

I am the sword in the darkness. I am the watcher on the walls. I am the fire that burns against the cold, the light that brings the dawn, the horn that wakes the sleepers, the shield that guards the realms of men.

GEORGE R.R. MARTIN

"We are all born with a divine fire in us. Our efforts should be to give wings to this fire and fill the world with the glow of its goodness."

ABDUL KALAM

Friends are like coals in a fire—together, they glow; apart, they grow cold.

C.S. LEWIS

Tradition is not the worship of ashes but the preservation of fire.

GUSTAV MAHLER

The mind is not a vessel to be filled but a fire to be kindled.

PLUTARCH

Which of these spark the most response? Why?

Anthrakia and Burning Away Shame

When they landed, they saw a fire of burning coals there, with fish on it, and some bread. Jesus said to them, "Bring some of the fish you have just caught."

JOHN 21:9–10

C uriosity draws me to the phrase *"fire of burning coals"* in John 21:9. The Greek word used here, anthrakia, is specific—it describes a charcoal fire rather than one fueled by wood. Charcoal burns hotter and longer, making it a valuable and intentional choice for creating fire.

Interestingly, the word *anthrakia* appears only one other time in the Bible. That's in John 18:18, where it describes the fire Peter warmed himself by as he denied being one of Jesus' disciples three times. (You can explore this moment in Matthew 26:69–75, Mark 14:66–72, Luke 22:55–62, or John 18:16–18.)

I wonder why Jesus used charcoal for the fire on this particular morning. Driftwood was likely available on the beach—easy to gather and sufficient for cooking breakfast. Yet the distinction of *anthrakia* seems deliberate. Why did Jesus apparently carry coals to the beach for this fire? Could there be a deeper meaning beyond making a good breakfast? Perhaps this fire was a subtle, intentional echo of Peter's earlier failure—one meant to reveal something dynamic and restorative.

A FIRE OF GRACE AND RESTORATION

In some significant and personal ways, I relate to sitting with the emotions of failure, guilt, and shame. For me, this scene carries a penetrating invitation to reflect on the weight of these emotions.

I believe Jesus crafts a subtle *trail marker* moment for Peter, one that embraces and guides me as well. Sitting by a fire of the same kind that accompanied Peter's denials, Jesus creates a space for healing and transformation.

Three times, Jesus asks Peter: "Do you love me?" Three times, Peter replies: "You know that I love you." And with each response, Jesus doesn't just offer forgiveness—He entrusts Peter with a mission: "Feed my lambs," "Take care of my sheep," "Feed my sheep."

There is a grace-filled beauty in this moment. Peter's three affirmations of love seem to redeem his three denials. The fire of coals, which once saw his shame, now becomes a place of forgiveness and restoration. But Jesus doesn't stop there. He moves beyond forgiveness to remind Peter of his purpose, reigniting his passion and compassion. This is grace at its fullest: forgiveness paired with a renewed vision of mission.

FIRE AS A SYMBOL OF EMOTION

In this story, fire becomes more than a practical tool—it's a symbol of emotional dynamics. Fire invites us to pay attention to what ignites our passion and compassion and to notice what cools or extinguishes our inner flame.

CONSIDER...

A time when you failed and then carried the weight of that failure with unwarranted shame or guilt.

A moment when you experienced grace, acceptance, belief, forgiveness that rekindled your passion and compassion.

A time when you created a "fire of coal" for someone else, offering warmth, belief, and nourishment in their space of struggle or failure.

REKINDLE

The fire on that beach wasn't just for cooking breakfast. It was a sacred space where guilt and shame were burned away, where forgiveness was extended, and where purpose was rekindled.

Sit with these two questions. Let the fire of coals remind you of the grace that restores, the passion that reignites, and the mission that calls you forward:

Where in my life might there be an *"anthrakia,"* a space where grace can restore what's broken?

How can I offer the warmth of such a fire to someone else?

Camped on the Edge of Hell

For as long as I remember I've been hurting; I've taken the worst you can hand out, and I've had it. Your wildfire anger has blazed through my life; I'm bleeding, black-and-blue. You've attacked me fiercely from every side, raining down blows till I'm nearly dead.You made lover and neighbor alike dump me; the only friend I have left is Darkness.

PSALM 88:15-18, THE MESSAGE VERSION

Early in Psalm 88, the writer proclaims, "I'm camped on the edge of hell." Weary, broken, hungry, thirsty, abandoned, sad, desperate, grieving...faced with a situation or circumstances I would do anything to escape. A dark night of the soul. I have dipped my fingers into the despair and it has crawled up my arms, over my shoulders and down my back. The despair is consuming me. I have had a few times backpacking where these words capture the experience, either for myself or for some trailmates.

Whether on the trail or in the rhythms of everyday life, I imagine you've experienced similar times where the words from Psalm 88 feel painfully familiar.

Now I invite you to read all of Psalm 88 in The Message version.

Notice a couple of things.

First, the ending.

No happy resolution. No sense of the hero will prevail. No triumph and delight will rule the day. The opposite. It concludes with the writer sitting in despair, with no hope and no companion other than darkness.

Second, the humanity.

Growling, unfiltered profane rage and hurt. Capturing what it truly means to be human. Confirming there are times and seasons when life feels unrelenting, when rage, and hopelessness overwhelm. And affirming it's okay to feel the depths of grief, confusion or anger, and that it's okay to not be okay.

Sometimes, we feel pressure to cover our pain with positivity. But perhaps we need to give ourselves permission to sit with the hard things. Perhaps instead of forcing a spoonful of sugar to make the medicine go down, we can linger in the heaviness and wander and wonder deeper into the emotions, life, and thoughts of Psalm 88.

When have I felt like I was "camped on the edge of hell"?

How did it feel to sit in that place?

When and why do I feel I have to pretend everything is fine?

What happens when I stop pretending everything is grand?

What do I learn about myself—and about God—when I allow myself to fully feel these moments?

When darkness feels like my only companion, who do I walk and talk and share life with?

What do I need from others in those spaces?

How do I respond when others invite me to walk with them in their Psalm 88 seasons?

The Psalm 88 moments remind us of our shared humanity, our need for others, and the depths of our own resilience. You are not alone in the darkness.

LECTIO DIVINA PRACTICE

I"Hello darkness my old friend..."
PAUL SIMON, "THE SOUND OF SILENCE"

Find Disturbed's version of "The Sound of Silence." Listen to it a few times. Let the words, music, and spirit of the song percolate in your heart and mind. Walk with it. Sit with it. Practice Lectio Divina with it.

Music can meet us in the depths of our emotions. The words, the melody and the raw emotion of a song can stir emotions and guide us into deeper reflection.

What songs, lyrics, or melodies resonate with my own Psalm 88 experiences?

How can I use music as a tool to process my emotions?

Hopelessness to Hope

Easter 1981. Orefield, Pennsylvania.

The previous September, I had driven a U-Haul truck from New Brunswick, Canada, to Orefield, Pennsylvania, to pastor a church that had split, leaving behind five people on a good Sunday—and two on most.

Bea and Lloyd were the lifeline of that little tan brick building perched along Route 309, just north of Allentown. The building was all-in-one—church, fellowship hall, and parsonage—simple and nondescript. Each Sunday, Bea and Lloyd would arrive in their old VW Beetle, unlock the doors, and sit patiently in a pew near the front. When the clock struck 11 a.m., they'd press play on a cassette recorder, listening to a recorded sermon. Then they'd pray, leave, lock the doors, and drive home.

They did this every Sunday—keeping the church alive.

On the first Saturday of September, I arrived in the parking field with my U-Haul, stepping into a space that almost everyone else had given up on.

As I got out, an elderly gentleman approached me, hand extended. "Hi, I'm Lloyd. I'm half your congregation," he said with a grin. I laughed. He wasn't joking.

Lloyd helped me unload the truck, and my family and I settled into the parsonage, where the living room was so small you could sit on the sofa against one wall and rest your feet on the opposite wall.

My daughter Laura's crib was set up in the foyer, leaving the back door as the only entrance for anyone attending a church service.

And so began an incredible year.

FROM TWO TO FORTY

Fast-forward past many incredible moments—lessons, challenges, joys, experiences, discoveries, and so much more. It was now Easter Week, 1981. What started as a congregation of five had grown to nearly forty—a beautifully ragamuffin group of cast-offs, skeptics, seekers, and perhaps a few angelic souls.

We decided to create a passion play for Good Friday and Easter Sunday. Our small but passionate troupe poured our hearts into retelling the story of Maundy Thursday and Dark Friday through the perspectives of Peter, Mary, and Jesus.

On Good Friday, Bruce—portraying Jesus with conviction—spoke the seven last statements from the cross. I played Peter and, with each statement, I pinched out a candle flame one by one. When Bruce solemnly uttered the final words, "It is finished," I extinguished the last candle, and the sanctuary was left in complete darkness.

In that dark space, I invited everyone to leave carrying the unresolved tension and weight of the crucifixion in their hearts and minds, and then to join together again for an Easter Sunrise service. Then silence. We all slowly walked out in the hushed darkness and despair and confusion, carrying the heaviness of that Friday.

FROM DARKNESS TO LIGHT

Early Sunday morning, we gathered again for the Easter Sunrise service. As we stepped back into the sanctuary, the space we had left in darkness was now filled with the scent of flowers and the presence of light.

An empty cross lay across the steps to the platform, surrounded by lilies. Hope replaced despair. Life bloomed where death had lingered. Passion and compassion reignited.

FROM EXTINGUISH TO IGNITE

What are the practices, experiences, or moments that cause the flames of passion and compassion in my life to flicker or burn out, leaving me in a space of growing despair, apathy and hopelessness?

What are the practices, experiences, or moments that reignite the sense of hope and the scents of aliveness in my life?breathe life into my? What fills you with hope, reignites your inner fire, and brings the scents of aliveness?

Extinguish...hmmm. My ponderings, explorings, and reflections:

Ignite...hmmm. My ponderings, explorings, and reflections:

A CANDLE...

From darkness to light, despair to hope, extinguished flames to reignited fire—this is the story of Easter. Let this trail remind you that even in spaces of hopelessness, there is a possibility of renewal, passion, and compassion waiting to be rekindled.

Where in life might there be a flickering flame ready to ignite anew?

LECTIO DIVINA PRACTICE

Dear end of your rope, dear worn out and broke...Amen on
behalf of the last and the least
On behalf of the anxious, depressed and unseen
Amen for the workers, the the hungry , the houseless

—SPENCER LA JOYE, "PLOUGHSHARE PRAYER"

Find Spencer LaJoye's song, "Ploughshare Prayer." Listen to it a few times. Let the words, the music, and the spirit of the song percolate in your heart and mind. Walk with it. Sit with it. Practice Lectio Divina.

Emotional Wellness

Life often feels like a swirl—a mix of experiences, challenges, and opportunities, each bringing its own blend of emotions. Emotional wellness is the ability to navigate and express those feelings in a healthy way. It helps us stay grounded in community, face life's challenges, and savor its joys.

There are many excellent resources available to help explore and nurture emotional wellness, and I encourage you to do some exploring. For now, let's reflect on one specific aspect of emotional wellness: the vital role of imagination, curiosity, and creativity.

IMAGINATION AND EMOTIONAL WELLNESS

When I ponder the idea of all people created in the image of the Creator, it nurtures a deep response and belief: We are all people of creativity and curiosity, fueled by the wonder of imagination.

I love how young children embody this truth. They infuse their days, their play, their learnings, and their interactions with wonder, curiosity, and the freedom to imagine endlessly. Their "why" questions—sometimes it seems like hundreds of them a day—are driven by an innate hunger to explore and create.

But somewhere along the way, the questions grow quieter. The swirl of life, along with cultural norms and pressures, often shushes curiosity and stifles imagination. This shift is sobering.

In 1968, researchers George Land and Beth Jarman conducted a study that tested the creativity of 1,600 four- and five-year-olds.

They used a creativity test designed for NASA to identify innovative engineers and scientists.

The results? **98% of the children tested at a genius level for creativity.**

Five years later, the same group was tested again. Only **30%** still tested at the genius level.

Five years after that, the percentage dropped to **12%**.

When over 200,000 adults took the same test, only **2%** scored at the genius level.

This research revealed a troubling conclusion: non-creative behavior is learned. Imagination, the natural capacity we all possess as children, is often drained and diminished as we grow.

RELEARNING IMAGINATION

If this capacity for imagination can be unlearned, then surely it can also be **relearned, refueled, and nurtured.**

Imagination fuels innovation. Curiosity fuels creativity. Together, they spark growth in every area of life—whether in technology, science, medicine, business, the arts, or everyday relationships. Cultivating imagination isn't just about play; it's a skill that transforms work, creativity, and connection.

A PERSONAL STORY: A CHRISTMAS CAROL

One of my lifelong favorite stories is *A Christmas Carol* by Charles Dickens. As a child with only one channel on our black-and-white TV, I eagerly waited each year to watch Alastair Sim's portrayal of Scrooge. It was a yearly tradition I approached with fervor and devotion.

Over the years, I've seen nearly every version of the story—films, theater productions, you name it. In the 1970s, I even directed a community theater production and still dream of one day playing Scrooge myself.

One experience stands out: seeing Patrick Stewart perform a solo adaptation of *A Christmas Carol* in London. With minimal props and set design, Stewart portrayed over forty characters from the story. He relied on Dickens' powerful text—and the imaginations of his audience—to bring the tale to life. It was a stunning reminder that sometimes, *less* is more.

Imagination invites us into these kinds of transformative moments.

REFLECTIONS

What were some of my favorite "make-believe" games or imaginative experiences as a child?

What role has imagination played in my life?

What nurtures the space and pace of imagination in my life today?

What dims or stifles the space and pace of imagination in my life?

An Exercise in Imagination

"What if imagination is not only a muscle we can stretch and strengthen, or a skill we can practice and hone? What if our imagination is also a sacred space where we can connect with ourselves, our ancestors, even future generations...a place where poetic knowledge can emerge."

RUHA BENJAMIN

"Imagination is the central formative agency in human society...It's because we can imagine different futures that we can struggle against the present state of things."

NGŨGĨ WA THIONG'O

"There is a difference, though, between delusion and imagination."

JEFF SHARLET

STREET HOCKEY AND IMAGINATION

Imagination is a key element of emotional wellness and a vital part of really living in the swirl of life. It opens the door to curiosity, creativity, and wonder. It rekindles my capacity to dream and hope. The future begins in the sacred space of imagination.

As a child I lived at 44 Princess Street in Moncton, New Brunswick, Canada. Just two blocks long, it is the shortest street in the city. But for me, 44 Princess Street was a portal that opened to a boundless world of wonder and countless childhood adventures.

At seven years old, I started playing ball hockey on Princess Street stepping right out the door of 44. I played with Tommy Weldon, Bimbo Harriman, David and Dougie Blackie, and other kids from the neighborhood. We played for hours under the sun or under the street lights. We played in the heat of the summer and the cold days of winter. Whether in sneakers or boots, t-shirts or parkas we played. None of those factors mattered. What mattered was imagining ourselves as our heroes.

For my best buddy Bimbo, it was Bobby Rousseau of the Montreal Canadians. For me, it was always #14, Dave Keon of the Toronto Maple Leafs. I scrawled his name and number on every hockey stick I owned and every game I imagined leading the Maple Leafs to thrilling victories. (Always against Rousseau and the "Habs" of course)

As I shared back in Trail 22, I continue to play ball hockey as I have entered into my seventies. And I still play with imagination. I spend more time stretching and preparing with exercise and diet then I did those early days. That is necessary to my commitment to still play with the passion and joy of my childhood. In similar spirit,

I also pay attention to stretching my imagination, nurturing it like a muscle to keep it vibrant and alive.

Let me encourage you to do the same: curate, craft, and protect your capacity for imagination. It's not just for childhood. It's a lifelong skill, a sacred space where you can dream, innovate, and reconnect with wonder. Imagination thrives in spaces where curiosity and joy are welcome.

Do some exploring into practices to improve imagination. Explore with reading and study but also explore by playing on a teeter totter, swings, and slides. Or find your way to the streetlight by 44 Princess St. with a hockey stick, a ball, wearing a pair of sneakers and a smile and.....

A little trail aside from my Field Notes: Two books I've found invaluable in keeping my imagination alive are *Imagination: A Manifesto* by Ruha Benjamin and *The Creative Act: A Way of Being* by Rick Rubin. Both are wonderful companions for wandering and wondering on this journey of imaginative exploration.

REFLECTIONS AND PRACTICES

Here are some quotes and ideas to reflect on. Take time to pencil your thoughts about what they suggest and how they resonate with you:

"We need to give the voice of the cynical, skeptical grouch that patrols the borders of our imagination a rest."

RUHA BENJAMIN

"Imagination is more important than knowledge."

ALBERT EINSTEIN

"Creativity is the superpower that we all possess...the most potent, transformative tool at our disposal. It is not the preserve of an elite few. Creativity is what humans do."

DAVID EAGLEMAN, THE CREATIVE BRAIN

"The theorizing and processing that happens in play helps children develop the skills and imaginative force necessary to confront oppressive ideologies that restrict their holistic development."

ARIANA BRAZIER, YEA I'M IN MY HOOD. NO STRAP.

"All children are born geniuses; 9,999 out of every 10,000 are swiftly, inadvertently degeniusized by grownups...We spend the first six years of their lives degeniusizing them."

R. BUCKMINSTER FULLER

"The important thing is to not stop questioning...never lose a holy curiosity."

ALBERT EINSTEIN

"We must tap the well of our own collective imaginations, as earlier generations did: dream. Call me utopian, but I inherited my mother's belief that the map to a new world is in the imagination...Sometimes, the conditions of daily life, survival, and temporary pleasures render much of our imagination inert. We're constantly putting out fires and

responding to emergencies, leaving little room to see beyond the present."

—ROBIN D.G. KELLEY, FINDING THE STRENGTH TO
LOVE AND DREAM

"I think we're way too focused on creativity. We should be focused on imagination. Creativity solves today's problems, but imagination sees a new world. If we can't imagine something new, we're stuck in the present. Art, music, and curiosity are critical, not formulaic thinking. We need imagination and curiosity to drive tomorrow's science and innovation."

JOHN SEELY BROWN

"Our culture can implement almost anything but imagine almost nothing. This royal consciousness that can achieve everything is the same one that shrinks imagination because imagination is a danger...The vocation of the prophet is to keep alive the ministry of imagination, conjuring and proposing alternative futures to the single one the king deems thinkable."

WALTER BRUEGGEMANN, THE PROPHETIC IMAGINATION

LECTIO DIVINA PRACTICE: MOONLILY

*"When we play horses at recess, my name
is Moonlily and I'm a yearling mare."*

MARILYN NELSON, MOONLILY FROM HOW I DISCOVERED POETRY

Find Marilyn Nelson's poem, "Moonlily." Read it slowly, a few times. Let the words and the spirit of the poem percolate in your heart and mind. Walk with it. Sit with it. Practice Lectio Divina.

Social Wellness

Social wellness is about the relationships and connections that nurture us and those we nurture in return. It's found in:

- Healthy relationships with the people we share life with—whether at work, school, play, with family, or even strangers in the grocery aisle or on an airplane.
- A sense of connection and belonging that anchors us beyond ourselves.
- Support and encouragement during the hard times when loneliness creeps in, threatening to consume.
- The stuff of healthy relationships, the small daily acts of interaction and compassion that nurture and breathe life into community.
- These are dynamics of social well being, reminders that life thrives when voices not only sing but actually live out, "Stand By Me."

THE GREATEST COMMANDMENT??!!

One day, as Jesus was being who he was and doing what he did, he found himself in the temple courts, surrounded by high priests, religious scholars, and leaders who challenged his being and doing. In response to the challenges, he told some stories and raised some ponderings.

In response to *that* response, one of the scholars asked Jesus, "Of all the commandments, which is the greatest?"

Whether it was a pick out of the 613 commandments in the Torah or the 10 Moses came down from the mountain with, we are not sure. Whether it was an attempt at stirring a rigorous GOAT (Greatest Of All Time) debate, we're not sure. But Jesus' answer was clear:

"Love the Lord your God with all your heart, all your soul, and all your mind. This is the greatest and most important commandment. The second is like it: Love your neighbor as yourself."

Jesus ties together passion for God and compassion for self and others. I like how love for the Creator flows naturally into love for the created. The compassion flowing out of the passion. I like how compassion for all creation flows out of loving self. Compassion for our neighbors is directly linked to how we love and care for ourselves.

I wonder: **Does nurturing practices like creativity, imagination, and curiosity—the emotional dynamic—help us better engage with crafting and curating community, civility, and neighborliness— the social dynamic?**

I wonder how we might nurture our well-being to contribute to the social well-being of others.

RECOGNIZING...IT'S ABOUT CONFIDENCE

Back on Trail 36, we sat by a fire and explored the dynamics of guilt, shame, grace, and forgiveness for a bit. Let's return to that story and find a moment that invites us to ponder dynamics of social wellness.

"Then the disciple whom Jesus loved said to Peter, 'It is the Lord!' As soon as Simon Peter heard him say this, he wrapped his outer garment around him and jumped into the water. The other disciples followed in the boat, towing the net full of fish, for they were not far from shore. When they landed, they saw a fire of burning coals there with fish on it, and some bread." John 21:7-9

This scene unfolds early in the morning. The disciples had been fishing all night. Even though it was the third time Jesus appeared to them after the resurrection, they didn't recognize him when he stood on the shore and called out to them.

- I wonder why.
- Were they too tired?
- Was it the fog or shadows?

Or maybe there was too much distracting noise—the waves, the oars, or their own voices?

But notice what happens in verse 7: John, the disciple whom Jesus loved, recognized and declared, *"It is the Lord!"* That recognition sparked everything that followed—Peter jumping into the water, the shared meal on the shore, and the impactful connections and conversations around the fire.

I used to think John was rather arrogant with his self-reference as *"the disciple Jesus loved,"* as though he thought of himself as some kind of teacher's pet or favorite. But I've come to see it from a new perspective. I like it when my kids say *"I'm the one Dad loves,"* not as a statement of *"Dad loves me more than others"* or *"I'm better than the rest of you"* or *"Dad loves me and no one else,"* but as a simple declarative affirmation that *"Dad loves me."* I want my kids and grandkids and family and friends to say with belief, *"I'm the one he loves."* It's not about boasting or exclusivity—it's about confidence.

That's what I see in John. He rested in the truth that he was loved. Isn't that what we all long for? To live with the confidence that we are deeply and unconditionally loved?

It is the posture Jesuit priest Anthony de Mello captured with his, "Behold God beholding you... and smiling." (Remember pondering with that posture on Trail 29? It's ok if you jumped ahead and are planning on going back to it...it's your pilgrimage).

THE POWER OF ONE VOICE

John saw a man on the beach through the early morning shadows, realized it was Jesus, and with his simple statement, helped the others recognize and respond to what was unfolding for them that morning—especially Peter.

Was it a sixth sense that helped John see Jesus?

Was the recognition enhanced by his confident embrace of the love of Jesus?

Was he just at the right time and place when there was a little more clear view in the morning light?

Pause here on the trail to wonder, to imagine the sounds, the smells, the sights, the emotions, the reactions, the meal, the conversations...everything that was swirling in and around as the scene unfolds. Step into that morning. Sit around the fire.

Feel the ache in the muscles from pulling the fish in.

Taste the charcoaled fish chased down with deep gulps of fresh water or sips of wine.

Hear the laughter of stories and memories rehashed. See the smiles as hugs are exchanged and kisses are planted on cheeks.

Sense the fullness and joy of life that morning. Share the space and pace around the fire.

Imagine. Wonder. Breathe.

In a significant yet simple way, it all transpired because one voice said, *"Hey, it is Jesus."* One voice recognizing what was happening and speaking a few simple words.

Crazy how trite a line like, "It only takes a spark to get a fire going" feels to put here. It's easy to dismiss such phrases as cliché, to brush it off. But clichés often endure because they hold truth, truth that happens over and over. I try to pay attention to the moments when I want to move past a ponder because it seems so trite. So I don't want to ignore the power of one simple spark to ignite. A single voice can ignite love, warmth, and connection in ways that ripple outward.

As Frederick Buechner said: *"The place God calls you to is the place where your deep gladness and the world's deep hunger meet."*

I like the image here of recognizing the intersection of passions and gifts and the areas of hunger...hunger for purpose, for companionship, for justice, for safety, for shelter, for inclusion, for forgiveness, for love

SITTING AROUND THE FIRE

What is the spark I bring to life?

What passions and gifts can I offer to bring light, warmth, or nourishment to a hungry world?

What do I notice as you look out from my "boat"?

What needs do I see?

What areas of pain or hunger call out to me?

How can I listen more deeply?

How can I see more clearly?

What can I say or do to bring healing, connection, or hope?

How can I nurture relationships that bring life to others?

Who might need me to "stand by" them today?

What simple spark can I ignite in my community?

MERCY IN ACTION

"Sin is the failure to bother to love."

JAMES KEENAN

"Mercy is the willingness to enter into the chaos of another."

JAMES KEENAN

"Showing mercy, one human to another, is messy. It's not for the fainthearted. It's not a simple gesture. It causes sleeplessness. Tests patience. Disrupts. Torments. Still, it changes everything. Relentless sin. Bountiful mercy.

JUDY KNOTTS

Social wellness calls us into this kind of messy mercy—the sacred work of loving and being loved, of standing by one another, and of creating spaces where everyone belongs

A Social Wellness Practice—Compassion

A queen-size mattress and box spring dumped in the woods. The *when* and *where* were obvious. They weren't there yesterday on my walk along the White River, but today, there they were.

The *who, how,* and *why?* Those questions mystified me—and, to put it politely, **torqued my gourd.** (A more raw profane phrase might better reflect the actual words and emotions swirling in my head, heart, and spirit.)

Someone had to go out of their way to haul these out of their home, off the highway, and deep into the woods. It must have taken deliberate effort. Yet, rather than disposing of them responsibly, they left them here.

Over the next couple of weeks, my anger and confusion grew.

My wild sanctuary had been desecrated. *Why? How? Who?*

Then came the additional question: *What should I do? What could I do?*

I didn't want to keep walking by, consumed by a desire to catch and punish.

I didn't want to ignore it and move on.

I couldn't figure out how to carry or drag the mattresses out by myself.

And so, I wandered and wondered. And I practiced.

I was reminded of this truth: The world is full of actual and metaphorical garbage. Exploitation, enslavement, injustice, and systemic *isms*—racism, sexism, ableism, and more—oppress, marginalize, and strip dignity from people and creation.

I felt the weight of hopelessness, alongside the persistent invitation to indifference.

The question hung heavy in the air: *What can I do?*

WRESTLING WITH THE OPTIONS

I don't know how to clean up the world or make it right. The problems feel overwhelming, and my abilities feel limited.

- *So, don't do anything?*

No. That's not an option for me.

- *Then attack everything and fix it all?*

No. That's not realistic.

Well, what about some of the pieces of trash, the beverage cans, the food wrappers left around the mattresses and along the trail?

Rather than grumbling about the litter and judging the people who left it, rather than just being self-aggrandizing that I don't leave trash and that I recycle, could I do something?

Yes. I could pick up trash. Bit by bit. Piece by piece.

This internal conversation played out for a couple of days before I reflected on the wilderness practice of *"leave no trace,"* and how it could be a more effective part of my daily walk in the woods. It reminded me that I could take it a step further: *"Leave it better than you found it."*

A SIMPLE PRACTICE: LEAVE IT BETTER

Now, as I walk through the woods, I continue to focus on the wonder and beauty. But as a tangible reminder to engage the world with compassion, I also keep my eyes open to find a few pieces of trash along the trail to pick up, carry out, and dispose of properly. The practice teaches me to accept my role in helping to clean up messes that I didn't create. One piece at a time.

COMPASSION IN ACTION

"Jesus went through all the towns and villages, teaching
in their synagogues, proclaiming the good news of the
kingdom and healing every disease and sickness.
When he saw the crowds, he had **compassion** on them,
because they were harassed and helpless, like sheep
without a shepherd. Then he said to his disciples, 'The
harvest is plentiful, but the workers are few. Ask the
Lord of the harvest, therefore, to send out workers into
his harvest field.'"
—Matthew 9:35-38

In this passage, the Greek word for compassion is *"splagchnizomai"* (σπλαγχνίζομαι). It doesn't describe a mild, tender, or soft-hearted response to injustice or need.

It conveys a much deeper, visceral reaction—a gut-wrenching response.

The word literally means, *"pitied them from his inmost bowels."*

It's the kind of feeling you get when confronted with something so unjust, so unfair, so wrong that your stomach twists, your chest tightens, and you feel sick.

But it doesn't stop there.

True compassion, as described here, also captures a deep desire to act. It ignites and fuels an action of response. W**hat I see, feel, and recognize compels me to right a wrong.**

REFLECTION: WHAT CALLS ME TO ACT?

What kicks me in the gut?

What makes me sick and tired?

What needs in the world do I weep over?

Compassion isn't just about feeling deeply. It's also about responding:

What does serving or meeting needs mean to me?

What, where, how, when, who, and why can I serve?

What compassionate act can I do right now

What steps can I take to respond?

THE PRACTICE OF COMPASSION

Compassion isn't always grand or dramatic. Often, it's found in simple, deliberate acts:

- Picking up a piece of trash left behind.
- Standing beside someone who feels alone.
- Listening to someone's story without judgment.
- Recognizing a need and offering what you can, no matter how small.

These small actions, rooted in compassion, help create ripples of healing, connection, and hope in the world.

As I walk this trail—both literal and metaphorical—I am reminded: **One piece at a time, I can help leave the world better than I found it.**

Inspired to Passion and Compassion

"The great problems call for many small solutions...though many of our worst problems are big, they do not necessarily have big solutions."

WENDELL BERRY

"It means if there is something wrong, those who have the ability to take action have the responsibility to take action."

BENJAMIN FRANKLIN GATES, NATIONAL TREASURE

MOVING FROM FEELING TO DOING

For me, some of the most powerful catalysts for passion and compassion come from the stories told through film and music. Certain moments have a way of stirring something deep within me—a gut-punch of truth or inspiration that moves me from simply *feeling* to actively *doing*. Hey, I love a good story, whether in poem, film, song, novel, conversation...whatever medium it takes. And yes, just like my grandfather James Bradley, there are usually some weepy eyes involved. The stories help me bridge the gaps between head, heart, and hands.

I often find myself reflecting on lines or scenes from songs and shows that strike a chord, ignite a passion, and gently (and sometimes not so gently) nudge me toward compassion. Sometimes it's the call to action speech of a William Wallace or Aragorn (a leader real or fictional), sometimes it's the simple but significant choice of an everyday character, or sometimes it's a stirring musical lick and lyric that captures my mind and heart at just the right moment.

REFLECTION...WHAT INSPIRES ME?

What are some movie or TV scenes and quotes that inspire me to passion and compassion—to action?

Is it the moment where the hero overcomes impossible odds? The quiet decision of someone choosing kindness over anger? The conversations that remind me of what matters most?

What songs are on my "inspire action" playlist?

Is it anthems that stir courage? Ballads that remind me of love's power? Lyrics that call me to be braver, stronger, more present?

A PERSONAL REFLECTION

Wendell Berry reminds us that the world's biggest problems don't always have big solutions. Often, it's the accumulation of many small steps of care, courage, and conviction that makes a difference.

In a similar vein, the quote from *National Treasure* speaks to our responsibility. It's not enough to notice what's wrong; if we have the ability to act, we're called to step in and do something—however small it might seem.

Movies, music, and stories inspire this response by showing us what's possible. They awaken something in us that calls us toward passion for what matters and compassion for those in need.

At the end of the day and at the end of the trail crafting a bit of space and pace to hear that call is my hope for every person I share a trail with.

Fire Campsite

eel the warmth, hear the crackle, watch the flames...you finished the Fire Element. Now imagine yourself finishing this section of the walk and setting up camp...your kitchen, your sleeping nook, your journaling/reading/yoga space...basically the campsite that gets on the cover of Backpacker Magazine.

We've reached our final opportunity to sit and reflect on a conversation around the kitchen circle. Just an extra wee bonus pulled out of the pack...perhaps a dark chocolate bar, perhaps a small bottle of Scotch. A chance to sit back, look into a star filled sky, tell stories, laugh, confess and share life.

FIRE CAMPSITE MOMENT: A HELPING HAND

On the trail there are moments when obstacles arise—a steep riverbank to climb, a rockfall blocking the path, or a narrow, demanding ascent. While you can navigate these alone, they're often easier with a helping hand. I love the posture of reaching down to help a trailmate overcome an obstacle. And I love it just as much when someone reaches out to help me. There's a joy in both giving and receiving help on the trail.

It saddens me, though, when help is offered but brushed aside with an attitude of self-reliance: "I don't need help. I've got this."

Too often, our culture rewards competition over community, independence over interdependence. Social media amplifies this, showing curated lives that shout, "I'm better, smarter, or stronger than you."

This mindset contrasts sharply with the communal values that have sustained many cultures throughout history. Hunter-gatherer societies, fishing villages, and farming communities relied on collaboration for survival. *"A cord of three strands is not quickly broken,"* as the old saying goes. Ambition and competition—especially at the expense of others—were rarely celebrated. Yet today, we live in a culture steeped in the opposite.

When we walk into a room—or scroll through social media— we often instinctively compare ourselves to others. *How do I rank?* We measure ourselves against others in smarts, skills, looks, and achievements. This drive to go it alone and prove our worth makes it harder to admit when we're struggling. And it makes it even harder to accept the helping hands extended to us along the way.

Yet, there is strength in vulnerability—in saying:

- "Here I struggle..."
- "Here I am weak..."
- "Here I need..."

Pause here and ask yourself:
How do I respond to the offer of a helping hand—physically, emotionally, relationally?

Do I accept it? Or do I resist, clinging to self-reliance?

Reflect on this bit of ancient wisdom from the book of Ecclesiastes:
Two are better than one, because they have a good return for their labor. If either of them falls down, one can help the other up. But pity anyone who falls and has no one to help them up. Though one may be overpowered, two can defend themselves.

A cord of three strands is not quickly broken.

FIRE CAMPSITE...REFLECTIONS, WONDERINGS, PONDERINGS, DOODLINGS

Feet warmed by the glow, eyes and ears captivated by the flicker of flames. As I explore the sparks, embers, and depths of being human—emotionally aware and thoughtfully present—what is revealed?

What makes my heart come **ALIVE**?

What makes my soul **SING**?

What moves my spirit to **DANCE**?

Onward and Onward

The Road goes ever on and on
Out from the door where it began.
Now far ahead the Road has gone.
Let others follow, if they can!
Let them a journey new begin.
But I at last with weary feet
Will turn towards the lighted inn,
My evening-rest and sleep to meet.
Still 'round the corner there may wait
A new road or secret gate;
And though I oft have passed them by,
A day will come at last when I
Shall take the hidden paths that run
West of the Moon, East of the Sun.

BILBO BAGGINS / J.R.R. TOLKIEN

We've reached the end of this journey, and like any trail worth exploring, it simply invites the exploring and discovery of more trails. But this is where I must put down my pen and resist the temptation to continue endlessly with more thoughts and stories. Instead, I simply say: **Thank you** for sauntering with me. I wish you **traveling mercies** as you continue your own journey. Embrace the discovery of new roads and hidden paths.

So, I leave you with:

A ponder,
A prayer,
A poem,

And...A pilgrim's story.

A PONDER

"The world is a dangerous place to live, not because of the people who are evil, but because of the people who don't do anything about it"

ALBERT EINSTEIN

"Every man must decide whether he will walk in the light of creative altruism or in the darkness of destructive selfishness"

MARTIN LUTHER KING, JR.

Are people like Mother Teresa and Nelson Mandela extraordinary people, or do they seem extraordinary only because of my own complacency, indifference, and selfish disregard for others?

The world I live in is full of selfishness and evil. But it is also full of incredible selflessness, of moments that inspire me to love and live fully. Everything I am and everything I offer comes from a being—heart, mind, and soul—that is both frightened and free.

A PRAYER

Feed me with the food I need.
Teach me to sow the seed of love.
Hold my hand when I walk alone and afraid.
Forgive me the evil I have done to Your other children,
and help me forgive those who have done evil to me.
When darkness surrounds me,
hold me in Your loving embrace. Amen.

A POEM

And what do I risk to tell you this, which is all I know?
Love yourself. Then forget it. Then, love the world.

MARY OLIVER, "TO BEGIN WITH, THE SWEET GRASS"

Find Mary Oliver's poem, "To Begin With, The Sweet Grass."
Read it slowly, more than once. Let its words and spirit percolate
in your heart and mind. Walk with it. Sit with it. Perhaps practice
Lectio Divina with it.

A PILGRIM'S STORY

Your story...SAUNTER into it.

Gratitudes

I am constantly amazed at the impact of walking with others, at how trailmates inspire me to live with passion and compassion. So deep thanks to the many many many who have walked with me, whether it be back country or front country, wooded paths, desert canyons, remote jungles, city sidewalks and alleyways. Your trust in me as a guide, your presence with me as a fellow pilgrim and your embrace of the elements and experiences encouraged me to explore the reality of this writing adventure.

I stepped onto the trail of writing Sauntering Homeward with naive enthusiasm and eagerness. Like any worthy trail, the reality of the rigors soon appear and challenge heart and mind. The journey is better with the wisdom, direction and counsel from experienced guides. Thanks to the guidance of my editorial team...Emily Sutherland, Ron Mazellan, Maria D'Marco, Lindsey Cornett and Elizabeth Caudle. I never would have finished this journey without your advice, attention to details and encouragement.

Family and friends...your belief and willingness to walk with me not just through this adventure but through the adventure of life amazes me along the path and sustains my steps. The depth of your grace, patience, kinship, smiles, tears as you share the walk with me cannot be measured but only experienced. You are the legacy of this adventure. And Kelly, thank you for your words to start me on this journey that December 5 evening. And then the willingness to walk with me every step of the way with your love and support and nurture. Much love...and let's go for a stroll.

Endorsements

———

"Larry Mitchell is a modern bard in the ancient Gaelic sense – blues shouter, story spinner, soul poet. A wanderer who has been lost often enough that he now has a pretty good sense of where he's headed. Better even than this, he's a guide and companion to other pilgrims, especially those a little less seasoned.

Larry is a recovering preacher; don't expect him to tell you how it is or what to do. He's a tender cynic, a gifted disorienter who will gently pry your fingers from the myths you cling to, spin you around a few times, then help you find the truer, more faithful path. You'll find you talk more than he does. He knows the wisdom of both words and silence – yours and his and God's. Walk with him. Listen."
— **Greg Paul**

"Larry Mitchell walks with everybody—everybody! Privileged people, street people, liberals, conservatives—he wants everybody to pause and see the world for the messed up, creative, hate-filled, God-loved place that it is."
—**Father Charles Allen**

"I would say that Grey Mitchell is one of the world's great educators, and this would be true enough, except that his craft results in more than an education. To walk (or sit and talk and eat and travel and work and play) with Larry is to experience an apprenticeship in how to live. And not just how to live with hope, purpose, and direction. Sure, all those things too. But gleaning from Larry's company and craft goes deep to the stuff of being human.

Grey is a spinner of the stories, symbols, and metaphors that hold space for the meaning we weave into our day-to-day lives. As an educator, communicator, companion, and guide he works these storied threads into shared experiences that amplify their impact. Larry shows you how to survive in an often confusing world, and how to channel your survival into contributing to a better world. He's also a great dad."
— **Aram Mitchell**

www.ingramcontent.com/pod-product-compliance
Lightning Source LLC
Chambersburg PA
CBHW011220120626
46545CB00010B/3075